Books that Saved My Life

ALSO BY MICHAEL McGIRR

Things You Get for Free
Bypass: The Story of a Road
Snooze: The Lost Art of Sleep

BOOKS
that
SAVED
My
LIFE

READING FOR WISDOM,
SOLACE AND PLEASURE

Michael McGirr

TEXT PUBLISHING MELBOURNE AUSTRALIA

textpublishing.com.au
textpublishing.co.uk

The Text Publishing Company
Swann House, 22 William Street, Melbourne, Victoria 3000, Australia

The Text Publishing Company (UK) Ltd
130 Wood Street, London EC2V 6DL, United Kingdom

Published by The Text Publishing Company, 2018.
Book design by Jessica Horrocks.
Cover images by iStock, Ralph Smith / Getty and Shutterstock.
Typeset by Typography Studio.

Printed and bound in Australia by Griffin Press, an accredited ISO/NZS
14001:2004 Environmental Management System printer.

The paper used in this book is manufactured only from wood grown in sustain-
able regrowth forests.

ISBN: 9781925773149 (hardback)
ISBN: 9781925774054 (ebook)

A catalogue record for this book is available from the National Library of
Australia.

For Chris Straford, 1961–2017
With love and gratitude

'I say more: the just man justices;
Keeps grace: that keeps all his goings graces'
—Gerard Manley Hopkins

CONTENTS

1 An Introduction...1
Harper Lee, *To Kill a Mockingbird* (1960)

2 Magic Words...10
Margaret Atwood, *Hag-Seed* (2016)

3 Living Memory...17
Baba Schwartz, *The May Beetles* (2016)
& Jacob G. Rosenberg, *East of Time* (2005)

4 Mostly I Wait...25
Tim Winton, *Eyrie* (2013) & *Cloudstreet* (1991)

5 Honest to God...33
Jeanette Winterson, *Why Be Happy
When You Could Be Normal?* (2011)

6 The Bottom of the Pile...39
Genelle Guzman-McMillan, *Angel in the Rubble* (2011)

7 Riddikulus...43
J. K. Rowling, *Harry Potter and the
Prisoner of Azkaban* (1999)

8 Because There Is Pain...51
Annie Proulx, *Close Range* (1999)

9 Long Time Shaving...55
Nelson Mandela, *Long Walk to Freedom* (1994)

10 Finding Centre...61
Thea Astley, *Reaching Tin River* (1990)

11 The Other Side of the River...68
Toni Morrison, *Beloved* (1987)

12 Large...76
Les Murray, 'An Absolutely
Ordinary Rainbow' (1969)

13 The Bedside of My Mother...84
Simone de Beauvoir, *A Very Easy Death* (1964)

14 The Freshness of Good...93
Hannah Arendt, *Eichmann in Jerusalem* (1963)

15 The Whole Story Is the Meaning...101
Flannery O'Connor, *A Good Man
Is Hard to Find* (1955)

16 Silent Voice...109
Thomas Merton, *The Sign of Jonas* (1953)

17 Sharp Elbows and a Hacking Cough...115
Dorothy Day, *The Long Loneliness* (1952)

18 Loss...121
Vera Brittain, *Testament of Youth* (1933)

19 Exquisite Moments...128
Virginia Woolf, *Mrs Dalloway* (1925)

20 Not of Ourselves...138
Mary Gilmore, *The Passionate Heart* (1918)

21 The Best of All Impossible Worlds...144
G. K. Chesterton, *Charles Dickens* (1906)

22 A Local Habitation and a Name...149
Joseph Furphy, *Such Is Life* (1903)

23 A River Somewhere...155
Joseph Conrad, *Heart of Darkness* (1899)

24 Love Came So Lightly...167
John Shaw Neilson, 'Love's Coming' (1896)

25 Unvisited Tombs...174
George Eliot, *Middlemarch* (1871)

26 An Old Tree...182
Leo Tolstoy, *War and Peace* (1869)

27 The Commander of an Army...188
Isabella Beeton, *Mrs Beeton's Book of
Household Management* (1861)

28 Ego Dismasted...196
Herman Melville, *Moby-Dick* (1851)

29 Reader, I Married the Wrong One...202
Charlotte Brontë, *Jane Eyre* (1847)

30 Lonely Creature...211
Mary Shelley, *Frankenstein* (1818)

31 Looks...220
Jane Austen, *Persuasion* (1818)

32 This Bed Thy Centre Is...228
John Donne, 'The Sunne Rising'
(early seventeenth century)

33 The Ingenious Gentleman...234
Miguel de Cervantes, *Don Quixote* (1605)

34 By Spells and Medicines...243
William Shakespeare, *Othello* (c. 1603)

35 Plenty...250
Geoffrey Chaucer, *The Canterbury Tales* (c. 1390)

36 How to Live...257
Seneca, *On the Shortness of Life* (c. 55 CE)

37 Monstrous Strange...264
Herodotus, First paragraph of
The Histories (fifth century BCE)

38 Souvlaki...269
Homer, Book 24 of *The Iliad*
(eighth century BCE)

39 My Tears Have Become My Bread...275
A taste of the Torah, the Bible, the Qur'an

40 The Way Home...287
Lao Tzu, *Tao Te Ching* (c. sixth century BCE)

Epilogue: Words that Don't Come Easy...293
A Word of Thanks...299

'There lives the dearest freshness deep down things'

—Gerard Manley Hopkins

CHAPTER 1

An Introduction

Harper Lee, *To Kill a Mockingbird* (1960)

At the school where I work, we run a special program in the depths of winter, immediately after the midyear examinations. We take our sixteen-year-old students to parts of the city they seldom visit, in order to ask them to think about justice in the broader community. Most of the students take their exams seriously and so, for quite a while, they will have been focussed on screens or desks about eighteen inches in front of their noses. It is time for them to look up and remind themselves that the world is a large and complex place, and our personal ambitions are only grains of sand on a vast beach.

I have been a teacher since Plato founded the academy and, in that time, have seen trends in education come and go, come again and go again. With each passing year, I am more convinced that the most important things that happen in a school are beyond easy measurement. We can be caught in a whirlwind of calibration, statistics, graphs, scores and results; and, like any gale, these are forces that play havoc with your hair, if not your whole head. I understand why we have assessment and standards, and I understand how clear standards often help less-gifted students. Nevertheless, a good deal of educational fine print is an expression of a deep anxiety, the rot that can drain schools of life. You have to remember there is always a person under all these numbers. Human beings do not always grow according to the progression points assigned by a bureaucracy. Nor do they ever grow without taking risks.

On one of our retreat days, I was with a delightful group of young men in inner Melbourne. Our program was simple. We began by sitting out in the cold for half an hour or so as the rest of the world was scuttling off to work, just watching the passing parade. Then we visited a centre that helps homeless young people. Our guide took us to several places where people sleep rough, and the students were surprised by how ingeniously they manage to hide themselves in a crowded city. Later in the day we visited a court to see justice in action for people at the raw end of life's deal.

One of our boys was Antonio. He was a great kid, otherwise I would hardly be bothered telling this story. His instincts were a little authoritarian but not unkind. He did not believe in safe-injecting spaces for the drug-dependent because, in his view, such facilities might encourage an unhealthy lifestyle. He wanted rapid solutions to youth homelessness. While he was one of those for whom the word 'crime' is never far from its shadow, 'punishment', he believed, like Plato, that education could solve many of the world's problems. He could articulate his point of view with clarity and tact, if not always a lot of empathy.

For lunch that day, we went to a vegetarian café run by the Hare Krishnas. It was a far cry from the Golden Arches, but—surprise, surprise—the students enjoyed the bean curry and mango pudding. Our conversation started with the encounters of the morning and soon moved to the recent examinations, because the boys had received their results for English. Antonio had one of the best grades in the year level of 260 students. He was understandably pleased with himself.

'Well,' I said, 'you clearly must have enjoyed *To Kill a Mockingbird.*'

The students had been required to read the famous book by Harper Lee (1926–2016), the only one she published in her lifetime. It has been a staple of high-school English since it was published in 1960, the year before I was born.

'Oh no,' he said.

'What do you mean by *Oh no?*'

'Well, sir, I never read it.'

I was flabbergasted. 'What do you mean, you never read it?'

'Well, sir, I started and got a few pages into it but decided I didn't like it and I didn't have time to waste on reading all those pages, so I just used the plot summary on Google.'

~

This is a book about why Antonio should have read—really read—*To Kill a Mockingbird*. It is a book about why he should still go ahead and read it, now that he is never going to face it in an examination but is only going to face the rest of his life, which I hope will be wonderful.

It is possible that, had he read the novel, his result in the examination might not have been as good. He might not have been able to make his argument with as much clarity and precision. His certainties might have been muddied by the novel itself. But clarity and precision are not the primary purposes of reading. *To Kill a Mockingbird*, like any great work of literature, has far more nuance than any plot summary, however detailed, can hope to provide. The thing that literature offers, not unlike our retreat day, is an experience of a broader world, one we can learn from but not control. Literature is, as my friend the poet Peter Steele (see Chapter 33) used to say, an engagement with the imagination of another human being. Reading is among the few communal activities that you do on your own.

Like programs of community service, literature has a significant role in helping people to develop empathy and compassion. These are not measurable commodities, but society is aching for lack of them. I teach in a world that is starving in spite of its own excess. Literature can feed people who are being left hungry by a culture that is all package and little substance. It is one of the luxuries we can't do without.

Deep in *To Kill a Mockingbird*, there is a description of Mrs Henry Lafayette Dubose, an intimidating pillar of the white Southern town where this drama of race relations plays out. Mrs Dubose is addicted to the morphine she uses to control pain. With the realisation of this uncomfortable truth, an imaginary border between respectability and its opposite comes tumbling down. Mrs Dubose's house is what you might call a safe-injecting space. There are a number of descriptions of her cold saliva, glistening around her mouth like ice.

At one point, Harper Lee notes: 'Her face was the color of a dirty pillow-case.' This is such a multivalent image that any synopsis is likely to overlook it. It doesn't add a great deal to the story. But it adds enormously to the texture of the storytelling, in ways that are difficult neatly to explain. A dirty pillow-case suggests a private life that isn't as orderly as Mrs Dubose believes the rest of the world should be; a face like dirty linen suggests that she reveals more of herself to the world than she would like. The image creates, for the reader, a new way of looking at a person and hence at the wider world. It is eye-opening. It also allows compassion for a woman who is lost in the folds of angry passivity—her spirit is bedridden.

I'm sorry Antonio didn't have the inclination, or make the time, for such slow reading: he missed out on a writer's craft that spins off in several directions at once. Harper Lee used an image that can help us, sixty years later, understand the drug-dependent around us without jumping to cut-and-dried solutions. This kind of writing asks you to look, to listen and to find a shared humanity.

There is another thing that Antonio missed out on. His life seemed to be moving in one direction. He had great ambitions for his future, and good luck to him. I am sure he will make a fine lawyer, especially if he bothers to read the relevant court documents. Perhaps one day he will be a judge and I will be hauled before him on charges of inconveniencing students with ideas of no cash value. But a full life is lived in two directions: backwards as well as forwards.

The current edition of *To Kill a Mockingbird*, a book that can sometimes be found lying dog-eared around our school, says on the cover, 'Over 30,000,000 copies sold.' My own books have sold somewhat fewer copies, so I am the first to assert that popularity is not always a measure of quality. Nor, for that matter, is unpopularity. But that many copies of a book in circulation give it a special status in our culture, meaning that all sorts of people have a relationship with it. It has become a kind of cultural bridge, something that enables people to reach each other over caverns and valleys. Giving such a book space in your life is one way of overcoming isolation. It helps you get off your island.

I recently taught a boy whose copy of *To Kill a Mockingbird* said on the cover, 'Over 5,000,000 copies sold.' His book was twenty-five million copies younger than the current one but it was exactly the edition I had when I was at school. I asked the boy where he got it.

'It was my father's,' he said. 'He had it when he was at school. It's his favourite book. He lent it to me.'

'Have you discussed it with him?'

'Yeah, he remembers every detail of it.'

'Have you enjoyed it?'

'You know what? It made me think about mob mentality.'

Here was a life moving backwards and forwards at the same time. In this case, the book had become a bridge back to his father's youth, and also to a future in which he was aware of the ways people get swept away by the mood of their community.

I had a similar experience when I chatted with a young woman on the desk at our local pool. She was reading a battered old copy of *The Lord of the Rings* with a yellow cover that I recognised from my own youth. She, too, had been lent the copy by her father and their love for it was something they shared. Another person serving on the counter at the place where my fourteen-year-old son buys computer games, a woman with a tide of tattoos rising above her collar, noticed I was buying a DVD of Father Brown, the most tweedy of all detective series.

'Oh, I love that,' she said, showing far more enthusiasm for my G-rated entertainment than for my son's latest version of *Destroy the Universe from the Comfort of Your Couch*.

'Really?'

'Yes, my grandfather introduced me to the original stories.'

G. K. Chesterton (see Chapter 21), the creator of Father Brown, would have laughed at this. He laughed at nearly everything. That's what made him such a serious writer.

~

There is an old adage that you won't go broke by creating fear. If you can make your customers feel inadequate in some way, they will buy whatever you can promote to relieve their symptoms, even if it's snake oil. This applies to every stage of life. Parents of infants can buy CDs of Mozart and Bach to improve the mental development of their children and help them get ahead of the pack. I have heard that students can buy CDs of Mozart and Bach to help them relax before examinations, and that businesspeople can buy CDs of Mozart and Bach to help improve their decision-making and optimise their workplace performance. Old people can buy CDs of Mozart and Bach to help them sleep and even improve their memories. I have wondered if these CDs all include the same pieces. Wouldn't it be better just to enjoy the music, whatever your stage of life, and let it take you to surprising places?

I hope this book might put something in the other column. It is a simple and heartfelt invitation to an anxious and defensive world—one increasingly prone to judge others rather than try to understand them—to join a quiet party. The party is a celebration of some of the books that have brought wisdom and pleasure to my life and the lives of many others. And solace, a word that we don't encounter as often as we need to.

Yes, I am thinking of young people like Antonio, who is now about to graduate from school. He is entering an exciting time of life: travel, career, friendship and hopefully new ideas. It is a time when people realise that the important things in life need structures and commitments to protect them. There's no point in saying you love your parents without making a commitment to be in in touch with them regularly. A career needs a structure and goals. Love needs an enormous outlay of time and unselfishness. Health needs decisions about diet, exercise and sleep. And so on.

Nobody is going to argue with any of this. You can find most of these ideas in fortune cookies and life-coaching seminars. The only difference between those two is that you can buy half a dozen fortune cookies for a dollar and at least have something to eat.

At every season of life, the mind needs to be nurtured. It needs challenges. Reading is as much a part of investing in yourself as are gyms, financial planning and relationships. It will feed your hungry mind and take your heart on a journey.

It will help you on the path of one of life's most elusive and hard-won freedoms, freedom from the ego. And it is never too late to start. This book is dedicated to a dear friend who was enthusing about a new book he had discovered in the days before he died. The book was not about death but nevertheless it helped with his journey.

This book is not a prescription. It rests on a belief that people often cope with a frightening world by hiding behind motivational slogans. We have much more to gain from finding a home for ourselves in complex narratives. Reading is not the only place to surrender to such complex narratives, but it has been the best one for me. I will talk about my connection with a certain number of books and, often enough, with the people and circumstances that brought them into my life. I have chosen forty or so texts that have enriched me; I could easily have chosen forty more, and forty after that. In each case, I have reason to be grateful for an extraordinary gift—a gift that is taking me a lifetime to unwrap. The excitement has never worn off. And I hope that one day Antonio might share it.

CHAPTER 2

Magic Words

Margaret Atwood, *Hag-Seed* (2016)

There's a four-letter word in the English language which is often referred to as the F-bomb. To be honest, it's not much of a bomb, being used so often that it's more like a squirt from a water pistol. Its origin is doubtful but not its meaning. Once upon a time, its use was an indicator of social standing. Now, like a tattoo, it has inked itself into all sorts of speech, pushing other more interesting words aside as it does so.

I once heard a teacher say to a recalcitrant student that instead of telling somebody to 'get fucked', it might be better to say 'go to hell.' She was assisting the child with anger management, and we all need help with that from time to time. Nevertheless, it did cross my mind that telling somebody to 'go to hell' was consigning them to darkness and despair for all eternity. Telling them to 'get fucked', on the other hand, is inviting them to have an experience of love. I can't see why the former should be considered more pleasant than the latter. Language is funny like that. We can't make rules without it and yet it doesn't seem to follow too many rules of its own.

I have noticed young people using the F-word as a crutch without realising how little support it actually offers. I have seen a boy in Year 6, aged eleven, use the word in the company of older boys, trying to impress them with his manliness. It didn't work. The older boys told him to F-off, demonstrating the correct intonation. The difference was that the older boys were more practised with their clichés. It is sad when people want to express themselves and have nothing but clichés with which to do it.

This is where Shakespeare can change lives. The common wisdom is that there are two Shakespeares: the one on the page and the one on the stage. They are both wonderful but being part of an audience with live actors is different from being on your own with a live imagination. There is a third Shakespeare as well, and this is Shakespeare in the classroom. It's not everybody's cup of tea. I once taught a young man who wasn't much interested in English but did love sport. Unfortunately, a dreadful accident at training left him in a wheelchair. He was determined to look on the bright side. 'At least it got me out of *Macbeth*,' he said when I visited him in hospital.

I have never had a student who didn't understand the story of *Macbeth*, even if some of them thought it must have been borrowed from the scenario of a computer game. Most of them understood the characters and themes. A good number

got the historical agenda of a Scottish king and others got
the gags: in the famous porter's scene, Shakespeare tells the
same phallic joke on seven separate occasions and each time
it's funny. Duncan is dead and the audience is waiting for the
body to be discovered so that mayhem can be unleashed upon
the world, but Shakespeare has some bawdy humour he wants
us to share first and everything else has to wait. Even with all
these attributes, *Macbeth* could still be a short story and make
the same impact. *Macbeth* is *Macbeth* because of the rolling,
crashing surf of its language. I want students to jump into that
surf and enjoy its energy.

My teaching has been aided by an entertaining resource
known as the Shakespeare Insult Kit, the work, apparently, of
a teacher in Indiana called Jerry Maguire. It has three columns.
You start with the word 'Thou', choose an adjective at random
from the first column, another from the second and pin them
both to a noun from the third. Presto.

Thou	cockered	fen-sucked	flax-wench
Thou	surly	nut-fed	rump hook
Thou	weedy	guts-griping	hedge pig
Thou	paunchy	hell-hated	maggot-pie

And so on. And on. Hours of fun for the whole class. Generally,
the students loved it and began to play around with strange
words. It was a bit like getting kids to try new flavours in
their food. For their homework, they had to use a choice insult
in a place they would otherwise be tempted to detonate the
F-bomb. Then they had to describe the experience. I got them
to write Shakespearean restaurant reviews and Shakespearean

sports commentary. Then they could make up their own bad words. If you liberate people's language, you are on the way to liberating them, and that's the whole point of teaching.

~

You often get the impression that the Canadian writer Margaret Atwood (born 1939) enjoys her craft. This is probably just as well because she was at it for years before *The Handmaid's Tale*, published in 1985, established her name. *Hag-Seed*, her retelling of one of Shakespeare's final plays, *The Tempest*, appeared when she was in her mid-seventies. It puts the lie to any idea that mature writers reach the point where they have had their day and their bones start to creak. *Hag-Seed* is a lot of fun. It is quirky and slick and nimble, and it does acrobatics to get the reader's mind moving. It has a healthy appetite for Shakespearean bad language.

You don't need to know *The Tempest* to enjoy *Hag-Seed* but, by the end, you will be hunting for a copy. The original drama tells the story of Prospero, the rightful duke of Milan, who has been tricked out of his position by his brother Antonio. Along with his daughter, fair Miranda, he is exiled to an island somewhere without the comfort of Club Med. Here he looks after Caliban, described in the cast list as a 'savage and deformed slave' and by Prospero himself as a 'demi-devil'. Caliban is the son of a witch, Sycorax, and possibly Prospero himself ('this thing of darkness I acknowledge mine'). The play begins with a storm at sea, conjured by Ariel, the fairy servant who does Prospero's bidding, which brings ashore Prospero's usurper, Antonio, as well as the king of Milan and the king's fetching son, Ferdinand, destined to marry Miranda.

This is a bland description: *The Tempest*, one of Shakespeare's shorter works, is a box of firecrackers.

Margaret Atwood centres her novel on a production of *The Tempest* by prisoners inside Fletcher County Correctional Institute. The director is Felix, a name that suggests prosperity, who was deposed twelve years earlier as the artistic director of the Makeshiweg Festival by a 'devious, twisted bastard' called Tony (Antonio). Felix's wife had died after a year of marriage, only to be followed by his daughter, Miranda, when she contracted meningitis, aged three. After a long exile in a remote shack, Felix reinvents himself as Mr Duke (get it?) and gets a chance to stage *The Tempest*, a long-held dream, even if he has to do it with 'thieves, drug dealers, embezzlers, man-slaughterers, fraudsters, and con men'. By the time the performance comes round, Tony and his cronies are wielding power in government. They come to Fletcher with the idea of closing down artistic programs that seem to be rewarding crime. Atwood turns them into the crew that comes onto Prospero's island. Like Prospero, Felix winds them up in his kind of magic and gets all the revenge he wants, plus a bit extra thrown in for good measure.

Theatre in general and Shakespeare in particular have had a fascinating relationship with prison. Prison populations famously have low rates of literacy, a reminder that crime, like weeds, often takes root in poor soil. Improve the soil and different things are more likely to grow.

Any English teacher would relish Laura Bates's book *Shakespeare Saved My Life* (2013). Bates started a Shakespeare program in the solitary-confinement unit of Chicago's Cook

County Jail. She was faced with the improbable situation, at least initially, of talking to a class from a chair in a corridor such that she could not see her students and they could not see her. Her class comprised men who had done horrible things and who had had horrible things done to them. Shakespeare had a role in breaking this poisonous cycle. She began with *Macbeth*, which has all the violence this crew was accustomed to. But *Macbeth* turns the habit of violence to which all of us can become inured by constant exposure back into something strange, frightening and alien. The prisoners responded in a visceral way that you don't get from students who basically want to know what is going to be on the exam. Bates's men were going nowhere. That is why Shakespeare took them places.

Atwood's *Hag-Seed* acknowledges Bates's book. One of the things that makes Atwood a brilliant writer is that she is such a generous and creative reader. *Hag-Seed* is not the first time she played with the pieces on someone else's chess board: *The Penelopiad* (2005) is a sassy retelling of the story not so much of Odysseus as of his wife, Penelope, who waited for him for twenty years on the rocky island of Ithaca while her bloke had adventures. *Negotiating with the Dead* (2002) is as fine a description of a writer's inner life as you are likely to find, mainly because it is as much about reading as it is about writing. Atwood is grateful for a childhood that included the two blessings often visited upon future writers: 'solitude and books'. She begins with a list of seventy-five separate reasons for writing that she has harvested from the insights of friends and other writers. A common theme is dealing with darkness:

Obstruction, obscurity, emptiness, disorientation, twilight, blackout, often combined with a struggle or path or journey—an inability to see one's way forward, but a feeling there was a way forward, and that the act of going forward would eventually bring about the conditions for vision—these were the common elements in many descriptions of the process of writing.

Atwood realises that the writer's business is often dirty. We need a lot more than a single lame curse to throw into the teeth of the gale.

In *Hag-Seed*, when Felix begins working on his production of *The Tempest* at Fletcher, he frustrates his cast by telling them that, if they want to swear, they can only use the curse words provided by the play itself. There is no shortage of these but they have to be found. Before long, the F-bomb is defused and replaced by expressions such as *toads, beetles, bats light on you, filth as thou art, abhorred slave, all the infections that the sun sucks up, hag-seed* and others beside. There is a moment towards the end when the cast is celebrating their triumph and eating food provided by Anne-Marie Greenland, who has played Miranda:

'These are poxy good,' says Leggs.
'She is one whoreson of a cookie baker,' says SnakeEye.

By this stage, you know that life has changed for these men and at least one aspect of their imprisonment is over.

If all the world is a stage, our role as the audience for the lives of countless others is to try to set them free from whatever chains or curse binds them. We have the magic words to do it.

CHAPTER 3

Living Memory

Baba Schwartz, *The May Beetles* (2016)
& Jacob G. Rosenberg, *East of Time* (2005)

Literature bears witness to the entire experience of the human family, however outrageous and however painful. There is scarcely a place where it has been afraid to go. There may be no such thing as a fearless writer but there have been plenty of fearless books. Literature often testifies to the understanding that pain can last a long time and that honesty doesn't take short cuts.

I was once asked to launch a book of poetry in Sydney by a writer who'd had a tough life. He'd been on the streets, been assaulted many times and resorted to drugs. His children had, for understandable reasons, learnt to give him a wide berth. As he tried to pull his life together, he wrote poems to give voice to his chaotic story. Some friends at a shelter decided to gather them up. They went to a copy centre and made a couple of hundred stapled copies, each with thirty-two pages. It was a modest publication in every way, and led to a wonderful cele-bration of life and survival at a launch where the local baker donated enough donuts to satisfy the most discerning literati.

The main thing, however, was that David's friends had applied for and got an ISBN, an International Standard Book Number. This required that two copies would be kept forever and a day in the National Library of Australia, which meant the world to a man with no permanent home. If his grandchil-dren, or their children, wanted to go looking for traces of him, they would find them there. His story would not be lost. This is one of the hallmarks of a humane civilisation. It is prepared to listen and to remember.

~

There is an ever-accumulating library of memoirs written by Jewish people in the aftermath of the Shoah, the Nazi catastrophe known as the Holocaust. May there be yet more memoirs to come. We live in a community with an uncanny ability to remember things that don't matter, such as some poor celebrity's wardrobe malfunction more than a decade ago. At the same time, we can forget the things that do. There are neo-Nazis gritting their teeth at us once again, intent on making their presence felt for reasons that beggar belief.

Of course, there is no guarantee that even the most heart-rending story will breach the defences of someone who is not prepared to hear it, someone whose sense of entitlement to their anger outweighs the entitlement of the rest of the world to justice and truth. But if any kind of literature has a chance of disarming the self-righteous, it is writing undertaken with unaffected honesty. Some of the books that recount the horrors of the Shoah have few pretensions to charming prose or silken imagery.

I met Jacob Rosenberg (1922–2008) when he was already an old man. For more than three decades, he had run a tailor's shop in Melbourne's Flinders Lane. He wrote Yiddish poetry. It took sixty years for him to produce *East of Time* (2005), but it is hard to imagine such a remarkable memoir being written faster. It is a work of long reflection and mulled pain. It tells a story which needed time to find the right words. Few accounts of inhumanity are as mellow as this one.

When Jacob arrived in Australia, soon after World War II, he brought with him a prodigious love of words and story-telling. He also brought memories of his time as a young man in the Jewish ghetto in Łódź, Poland, and later as an inmate of concentration camps, including Auschwitz.

East of Time is the first volume of Rosenberg's reminis-cences and brings the story up to the moment in August 1944 when young Jacob, who might have slipped away to safety, chose to remain with his family and join them for 'resettle-ment'. He could have guessed what he was in for. In the Łódź ghetto, resettlement notices were known ironically as 'wedding cards'; 'resettlement' was 'a virtual euphemism for murder'.

Despite its dramatic last moments, this is not a linear account. It prefers to call to mind, one by one, some of the colourful characters who shared the ghetto. Even before the war, people lived cheek by jowl. Rosenberg's family occupied a four-storey tenement with fifteen other families. Each family had a single room. Then, once the ghetto was established,

168,000 people were herded into an area of four square kilometres. They could hear each other's stomachs growl. It is a
tribute to Rosenberg's skill as a writer that he is able to create
room for individual personalities to flourish.

Among those personalities is Simcha. Jacob's father,
Gershon, was a Bundist and Jacob was brought up as a socialist,
albeit one who was taught to respect the practices of others.
His father refers to them as 'Yiddish socialists'. One year on
Rosh Hashanah, Jewish New Year, Jacob made his first visit to
a synagogue to hear Simcha intone the chant 'Avinu Malkenu',
meaning 'God is our father'.

The story then jumps ahead several years. In November
1944, Jacob saw Simcha in one of the labour camps. Simcha
had been employed to sing to the guards but, too worn out
to continue, was listed for the gas chambers. The deputy
commandant ordered him to sing a corruption of a popular
song of the time: 'This Is My Final Day'. Simcha refused. But
as the truck pulled away, he stood and sang 'Avinu Malkenu'.

Rosenberg lets a powerful story speak for itself. He
remarks that, this time, Simcha was singing 'beneath the
unblemished blue of an indifferent cosmic cupola'. His words
bring to mind the famous scene where God is put on trial in
Elie Wiesel's *Night*, published in Buenos Aires in 1956 ('I was
the accuser, God the accused').

There is, incidentally, another moment in Jacob's story that
does not appear in *East of Time*. In 1948, Rosenberg saw the
Nazi guard in the Melbourne General Post Office. I asked him
how he responded to such an encounter. 'Michael,' he said with a
characteristic shrug, a movement of his shoulders that indicated

everything other than indifference. 'Michael, there is a point at which you have to let the hatred go before it kills you, too.'

Much of Rosenberg's storytelling, like a good deal of the short fiction that appears in his earlier collection *Lives and Embers* (2003), is in a Talmudic tradition. It instructs by irony, subtle twists and distilled wisdom. Shortly before he too vanishes, one of the Rosenbergs' neighbours, Mechel Schiff, remarks to Jacob's father that 'language is the physical manifestation of man's spirituality.' The characters in this book never lose their hunger for deeper realities, even when they have been reduced to a parody of human living. The Jewish psyche, says this Mechel Schiff, is 'a spirit born of a marriage between exile and promise'. He says that the word 'remember' appears 169 times in scripture. At the end of this conversation, Rosenberg adds plaintively, 'we never saw him again.' This is typical of the movement of characters through his narrative. They deliver enduring wisdom before being treated like disposable goods.

On 12 February 1940, a cold day, Jacob recalls watching his fellow Jews as they dragged themselves into the ghetto. One in particular stays with him. Michael Rosz was pushing a cartload of books, a gesture of real defiance. Rosz was never going to be reduced to his bodily needs. As he lay dying, with the temperature outside eighteen degrees below zero, Rosz refused to burn his books for warmth, even to save his life. 'A Jew who burns his books might as well burn himself,' he says. 'Books are living things.'

~

There are not many survivors left. In April 2017, I was able to accompany about a dozen of our Year 10 students to the

Yom Ha'Shoah Commemoration Assembly at Mt Scopus College, a school with a long Jewish heritage. This is the sacred moment of the year in which the Mt Scopus community remembers in a special way those who died in the Shoah. It is rare for a non-Jewish school such as ours to be invited to share this experience, and the invitation we received owes a great deal to the bridges built between us and other traditions by my friend Chris Straford (see Chapter 14). It is not easy to describe the experience. It was a privilege, but that word gets used too often and does not stretch to cover a situation of such pain. We were fortunate to be there, but there was little that was fortunate about the stories we heard.

The main speaker for the afternoon was Baba Schwartz (1927–2017), a woman approaching her ninetieth birthday. She was accompanied to the stage by her son, Morry. Baba shared a story that none of us is likely to forget. As the survivors become older and fewer in number, I hope my students might pass it along to their own children and grandchildren. Baba's story of what she calls 'the great darkness' took us into a bleak chapter. Baba is one of those people, though, who can use darkness to make light.

Aged sixteen, Baba, her parents and her two sisters, Erna and Marta, were deported to Auschwitz. Her childhood had been spent in blissful simplicity in the Hungarian village of Nyírbátor. In her memoir of the first twenty years of her life, *The May Beetles*, Baba describes the ancient and humane rituals of her culture, such as those attending the courtship of her parents, Gyula and Boeske. The contrast between this world and what follows is dreadful. Seventy people at a time were packed into cattle wagons for a three-day journey to Auschwitz. On arrival, they were greeted by the infamous Dr Mengele. Boeske and her daughters were separated from Gyula, who was never seen again.

Throughout the ordeal that followed, Baba never gave in to despair. The day before the war finally ended, she still had no roof over her head: 'We settled on our backs and gazed up at the heavens, where a million stars glittered. I found myself smiling at them, blessing their beauty. I was still smiling when I fell asleep.'

When the four women returned to Nyírbátor after the war, they found that only 130 people had survived from a Jewish community of over three thousand. But Baba would not be vindictive: 'I recalled that, as we left Nyírbátor all that time ago, I had sworn to have my revenge. Now I had returned, and my revenge was that I was still alive. My life would go on.'

The undisputed heroine of Baba's recollections is her mother, Boeske. Baba tells the story of their arrival at Auschwitz. Like so many others, Boeske and her daughters were taken away to have their heads shaved and their clothes confiscated, and to be dressed in humiliating rags. When Boeske saw her three beautiful daughters in this new guise, she burst out laughing. They looked so ridiculous. Yes, she also cried. But it took a mother to laugh at this moment. Her laughter helped them to hold on to their status as human beings. It kept them going. It is a blessing to have people who know how to laugh at us when that's what we need.

Boeske is an extraordinary figure of freedom. It was she who orchestrated their escape into the woods from a death march. It was she who insisted that they return to the village. On their return, she remarried, partly so her daughters would not need to look after her. She wanted them to have their own lives.

Boeske seemed to know when to laugh and when to push; she knew when to hold on and when to let go; she knew when to take a risk. After seventy-five years, her legacy was alive on a grey afternoon in Melbourne in the living witness of her elderly daughter, helped to the stage by her own son, and heard by an audience of hundreds. During the assembly, the gathering remembered the victims of many other attempts at genocide, a chilling list. Yet Baba Schwartz said: 'There only needs to be a small complement of goodness in any person to turn him away from all the evil things he might imagine.'

I wrote to thank Baba and she signed a copy of her book for me on the day before she died, a month later. It is a precious volume, a tangible link to the story she found the freedom to share.

I have seen a replica of *The Diary of Anne Frank* (1947), an account of a young girl hiding from the Nazis in Amsterdam before she, too, was packed off to the camps, where she died in Bergen-Belsen aged sixteen. The diary was later found among the rubble left behind. I was astonished because, with its red cloth cover and clasp, it looked very much like a diary that my daughter, Clare, used to write in. Clare, now aged thirteen, often writes in the privacy of her room after she has been told to go to bed. Her clothes may be strewn all over the floor but I know she is giving order to her thoughts and making a place for her memories. Part of me would love to know what she writes. But I probably never will. I am just thankful that she does it.

CHAPTER 4

Mostly I Wait

Tim Winton, *Eyrie* (2013) & *Cloudstreet* (1991)

I have many reasons to be grateful for *Cloudstreet* by Tim Winton (born 1960). It was the first book I ever reviewed for publication. Since then, it has been followed by more than one thousand other books and, looking back on that review I wrote for *Eureka Street* almost thirty years ago, it strikes me now as high-falutin' twaddle.

Cloudstreet created a part-time job for which I am extremely thankful. Tim Winton himself once told me that he has never read a book without learning at least something and I would heartily agree with that, even if my learning has sometimes been modest. Reviewing has brought me into contact with writing I would never otherwise have experienced. It is where I have done some of my best listening.

Another reason for my gratitude concerns a woman

called Jenny Scott who, when young, left Australia and went to live in England for a list of reasons that did not include escaping me, as we had not yet met. She found kindred spirits in an offbeat Christian community in North London, part of whose vision was expressed in an annual arts festival called Greenbelt, held over the bank-holiday weekend in what the English refer to as summer. After *That Eye, the Sky* (1986) was published, Tim Winton made an appearance at Greenbelt and the community was struck by the depth of this affable, witty and intelligent young Australian with long hair and a poor wardrobe. The first meeting 'was a moment of instant mutual species recognition', says Tim. 'One sniff and we knew—evangelical leftovers!' He made friends: one member of the community, Malcolm Doney, makes a cameo in *The Riders* (1994).

When Jenny Scott arrived, the community urged her to read *Cloudstreet*, Winton's then most recent book. The novel reawakened for her a love of reading that she had lost sight of as life threw any number of unreadable challenges in her direction. She inched through the book standing in crowded trains on the tube during a dark winter, pausing when the light wasn't good enough to see the words on the page.

Cloudstreet is joyous. It is full of both sunshine and shadow, one of the reasons it has a place among the most popular novels ever written by an Australian. The book made Jenny Scott think more kindly of a country from which she had fled. In some ways, it was the beginning of her journey home. Without that journey, we would never have met. Our children should be grateful to *Cloudstreet*, too.

Jenny's experience encapsulates some of the magic of *Cloudstreet*. It is a book about home written by someone who was far from home.

Tim Winton was still a teenager when he made the most profound commitments of his life. One of them was to become a writer. Another was to feed his spirit on the landscape of his native Western Australia. These two commitments have been closely interwoven. Not long after *Cloudstreet* appeared, I was able to visit him in the basic fibro shack he and Denise, his wife, owned in a coastal town, a place Winton once described as 'plug ugly'. It looked like a puff of wind might blow it over. The whole house didn't seem to weigh as much as the ageing four-wheel-drive that stood outside. The garage had been converted into a workspace that Tim shared with a collection of well-used fishing equipment.

To an outsider, it might have looked as if Winton was on permanent holiday. This would be to miss the hard work and discipline he has brought to his craft, and the intent with which he honours the life of the mind. We became friendly over a shared interest in theology, especially the monk Thomas Merton (see Chapter 16). We also both enjoy novelists of the American South, such as Flannery O'Connor (see Chapter 15), Walker Percy and Frederick Buechner.

We went out on his small boat, a tinny, and Tim threw himself into the water while I held on to the side, hoping not to fall out. He later suggested that my life would be happier if it was more physical. He was right. I was a priest at that stage, which was no excuse for being sedentary.

Tim's creativity is tied to the physical world and he loves

the point at which the ocean meets the land. That meeting has fed him since his family moved to Albany, on the south coast, when he was twelve. He respects the natural world: I have been with him in a restaurant where he was uncomfortable because there was a fish on the menu whose stocks had been depleted by over-fishing. The ocean is ubiquitous in his imagination. He has campaigned on behalf of saving Ningaloo Reef. When our first child, Benedict, was born Tim sent us a card to celebrate 'a great catch on light tackle', a compliment Jenny enjoyed. In an essay called 'The Wait and the Flow' in the collection *The Boy Behind the Curtain* (2016), Winton has compared the life of a writer to that of a surfer:

> I come to the desk every day and mostly I wait. I sit for hours, bobbing in a sea of memories, impressions and historical events. The surfer waits for swells, and what are they but the radiating energy of events across the horizon, the leftovers of tempests and turmoils already in the past? The surfer waits for something to turn up from the unseen distance and if he's vigilant and patient it'll come to him. He has to be there to meet it. And when it comes he has to be alert and fit and committed enough to turn and ride that precious energy to the beach. When you manage to do this you live for a short while in the eternal present tense. And the feeling is divine.
>
> That's how I experience writing, which is its own compulsion. I show up. I wait. When some surge of energy finally arrives, I do what I can to match its speed.

Cloudstreet was mostly written at a time in the late 1980s when

Tim and his young family were overseas and he was missing the places that provided his orientation in the world. An arts grant had enabled them to live for a while in Ireland, Greece and Paris. This is where he worked on *Cloudstreet*, writing the novel longhand, a practice he has continued, often sitting in cafés to find space to work, even when that meant coping with the cold in Paris and the heat in Greece. Writing longhand has its drawbacks. When Winton got off the bus at Rome airport to finally return to Australia, he had left the one copy of the eight-hundred-page manuscript behind. He didn't expect to see it again and was returning to Australia with nothing to show for all that work. Luckily, a stranger had found it on the floor of the bus and gone looking for the author in the airport. The kindness of strangers is one of the themes to which Winton's work often returns.

Cloudstreet is nostalgic in the best sense: it longs for both a time and place that the author is missing. It belongs with James Joyce's *Ulysses* (1922) and George Johnston's *My Brother Jack* (1964) as a meticulous and detailed recreation from memory of a place from which the writer is absent, even in exile. This, I am sure, is what engaged Jenny Scott at a deep level as she discovered the book on the London underground. It helped to send her in search of home.

Cloudstreet is based around the Swan River and is a celebration of the Perth of the generation of Winton's grand-parents, and, indeed, some of the most eccentric happenings in the book are close to fact. It is richly comic. Even its language hankers for things past in delightful ways. There are expressions such as *doogs, staggerjuice, zacs, deaner, drongo, hittin the*

sauce, having the painters in, a bit of the foldin, pushin yer luck,
fair whack, donkey yacker, fourbetwo, fair dinkum and *dills.*

~

Tim Winton has never tried to write *Cloudstreet* again, although
he must have experienced pressure to keep the laughs coming.
The book steadily consolidated its place in Australian culture and
one of his young relatives ended up withdrawing from a course
in order to avoid studying *Cloudstreet*. Tim says: 'I think the book
(and probably its author) cast too big a shadow at the time.'

Tim found other fish to fry and his career, now in its
fourth decade, has always been open to new challenges. Those
challenges, like *Cloudstreet*, have often come from concern
about the vacant moral centre of the community he is part
of. In 2013 *Eyrie* was something to celebrate, not least because
it was the work of a writer who had continued to grow and
whose craft had only sharpened.

Eyrie is as different from *Cloudstreet* as then is from now.
Eyrie is a work of toughened wisdom. Many of the sentences in
it are as sharp as glass.

Tom Keely, the central figure, has reached the point that
Dante described, in Clive James's vernacular translation of *The
Divine Comedy*, as 'the midpoint of the path through life'. He
owns a small flat on the tenth floor of The Mirador, a charm-
less and barely functional architectural eyesore perched on the
edge of the continent in Fremantle, a part of Perth that prides
itself on not being part of Perth. Keely is forty-nine. Two
years ago, his marriage to Harriet fell apart. One year ago, he
suddenly lost the prominent job he had as a spokesperson for
an environmental agency.

For fifteen years, Keely had worked passionately for a cause in which he believed until a sudden 'brain snap', lasting about five or six minutes but which we never see fully dramatised, makes him a pariah. So it is that in the middle of his life he is left with a modest pension (which arrives on a day Winton describes as 'the fortnightly full moon') and a crumbling sense of self. Keely is a character sharply at odds with the myth of male ego which governs a good part of Australian culture. He is a mess made as much by the rapaciousness of his world as by his own hungers.

This is Winton's most pointedly political novel and it arrived during Western Australia's minerals boom, the 'endless reserves of mining loot'. His city is 'a philistine giant ready to pass off its good fortune as virtue'. Winton's excoriation touches everything from supermarkets to café society. The hungry are said to 'eat like pokie machines'.

Eyrie makes reference to figures as diverse and passionate in their views as Calvin, Bonhoeffer, Stanley Spencer and Billy Graham. Its lexicon includes expressions such as *shriven, redeemed, salvation, mercy, prayer, deliverance, fierce saviour, Great Defender* and so on. Keely's father, Neville, was a born-again minister intolerant of social niceties. He was one of God's strongmen, who stood up to a domestic abuser in their neighbourhood. Keely is his heir, at least in disposition, but he now has a hole in him where the Great Defender used to be: 'sometimes it was the size of him entire.'

None of this is to imply that *Eyrie* is a religious tract. But it is enthralling to see a writer blunting the sharp edge of contemporary culture with such a hard stone as intelligent theology, which is far from the self-righteous mush that generally gets passed off as the religious contribution to public debate. In some respects this is a jeremiad, albeit lightened by Winton's mischievous wit and his uncanny ear for dialogue.

Eyrie tackles myths of prosperity and success in a way that is not always comfortable but that stirs thought. It is rich in compassion and affectionate towards the unlovely. It has a strong belief that no journey ends at the halfway mark. It shares that belief with *Cloudstreet* just as much as both books share the Swan River.

~

When *Dirt Music* was published, in 2002, the cover of the book was reproduced on a full front page of the arts section of the *West Australian*. It was a major event, with an accompanying CD and much publicity, an aspect of his career Tim does not relish. By now Tim had an enviable rapport with a wide readership; he was as much a celebrity as a writer ever gets to be in Australia. I happened to be in Fremantle and we went out for a coffee. Tim asked if he could sit with his back to the café but people kept coming up to say hello.

This was a challenging time in my own life and Tim immediately disengaged from the literary world to listen to my problems.

'Just go to the light,' he said.

I asked what he meant by that.

'I'm not sure,' he said. To use one of his own literary expressions, he laughed like a drain. 'I'm really not sure. That's why I'm writing all these books. I'm trying to find out.'

CHAPTER 5

Honest to God

Jeanette Winterson, *Why Be Happy
When You Could Be Normal?* (2011)

Imagine a world in which only strangers were allowed to speak at your funeral. The person I would choose is Jeanette Winterson (born 1959). This is not just because I know my friends would enjoy her glorious accent, one which swings off final consonants like an acrobat. Reading an audio book of *Why Be Happy When You Could Be Normal?* she seems alive to every syllable she writes, even the painful ones which others might be tempted to skate over. She uses many short sentences but they drill deep. Yet the real reason I would choose Winterson as my stranger-eulogist is the generosity she brings to describing even those people who have hurt her. She takes risks just to understand. I salute that from the hiding place to which I often retreat, that of judgement.

Winterson and I would seem to have little in common.

She is from the industrial north of England, was adopted as a baby, and was brought up in a strange and loveless environment. She is a lesbian. I encountered her when I was aspiring to become a priest and read her first novel, *Oranges Are Not the Only Fruit* (1985), which, based on personal experience, describes her journey to extricate herself from the clutches of a deadly and sex-denying religion. Parts of it have a tender and lyrical eroticism. Every corner of my soul was barracking for her because she was on a journey to freedom and I hoped I might be on a similar journey, however different our two paths may have looked.

My reading life has often been enlivened by writers whose world is remote from mine. In the 1980s, I spent a few days in a slum in central Java staying with the then venerable priest and novelist Romo Mangunwijaya. I was homesick for the sweet-smelling suburbs of home. Romo Mangun showed me around the squatter settlement that was his home and explained how people buried anything they had which might be of value. Normally this would mean pictures and small statues, perhaps some documents. When the authorities came through and bulldozed the settlement, a pointless activity that happened every couple of months, people could return after the carnage and salvage their few precious items. On these occasions, he would bury his Bible and rosary beads as well as the manuscript of his work in progress. He was part of his community, not superior to it. This meant sharing the tough times.

He told me in faltering English that there was no such thing as a truth which left things the way they were. Truth is something we all grow into. I wrote those words on a card and buried them near his house, hoping one day I might return. I have done so many times, at least in my imagination. Romo Mangun was a trained architect who had chosen to spend his life with the homeless. He was comfortable with paradox.

I felt a similar connection with the writer, musician and radio presenter Eddie Ayres. We got in touch when he was still Emma Ayres, because we had enjoyed books that each other had written. Emma Ayres' *Cadence* is a delightful travelogue by a viola-playing lesbian, covered in tattoos, who rode a push-bike from London to Hong Kong, sharing music with some of the least harmonious parts of the world. My *Things You Get for Free* is a more timid travelogue by a person covered in godly confusion. We met in a coffee shop and talked for ages. I felt an instant connection. This was probably aided by the fact that I often heard her voice on morning classical radio and that she had a habit of choosing music that helped my son, who was in the car with me, get to school at a time in his life when that felt to him like a bike ride from one continent to another.

Later, Eddie wrote a book about transitioning from being a woman into a man, *Danger Music*, set in the context of teaching music in Afghanistan. I struggled with Eddie's story, possibly because I have had enough problems becoming a man myself. I continue to struggle with people changing gender, but accept that it might not be as great a change as using music to turn a stony culture into one of flesh. Eddie Ayres has helped me a lot, because I cannot doubt his honesty and his prepared-ness to pay a price for living out that honesty. He found a truth that changed him. That can be scary for others to witness. He could have chosen a far easier path.

So it is with countless writers who have rattled my orthodoxies.

So it is with Jeanette Winterson.

Why Be Happy When You Could Be Normal? is riotous; its darkest moments are as funny as a fart at a funeral. Wacky as it may seem, the title is a verbatim quote from the woman who adopted Jeanette as a baby and who is invariably known in the book as Mrs Winterson. She is the kind of loveless neurotic who has little idea how destructive she is and how much her idea of virtue is, in fact, the opposite. Her world is constrained by the mores of Elim Pentecostal Church, which is actually a couple of terrace houses in Accrington, a small town about twenty miles north of Manchester. She is the mother from hell—which is ironic because that is where Mrs Winterson thinks everybody is going, most of all poor Jeanette. She thinks that the only treatment for lesbianism is exorcism. After waging a bizarre guerrilla war against her adopted daughter, she concedes defeat and Jeanette leaves home. Mrs Winterson's last exasperated words to her as she goes out the door are, 'Why be happy when you could be normal?'

For all its dry earthiness and comedy, this book is about the pursuit of happiness—which means, for Winterson, as it did for Aristotle, the pursuit of truth. It is a minor miracle that Winterson, having grown up on a starvation ration of both love and honesty, should navigate both these reefs with delicacy. There are a number of broken relationships along the way but Winterson usually points to herself as the person responsible. She never suggests she would be easy to live with. The book includes an extraordinary account of depression and possible suicide, events that took place after *Oranges Are Not the Only Fruit* had been not only a successful novel but a hit in its TV version. It seems that not even that book laid Mrs Winterson to rest. Her legacy was permanent and Winterson had to make peace with that. Finally, there is a search for her birth mother.

There are at least three things that contribute to Winterson's humane sanity. The first, to borrow an image from the diet that got Winterson through the time after she left home and had to sleep on the back seat of an old Mini, is that she didn't throw out the hot chips with their greasy paper wrapping. She excoriates the church community she was chained to but still recognises 'the camaraderie, the simple happiness, the kindness, the sharing, the pleasure of something to do every night in a town where there was nothing to do'.

The second is that she was able to throw out the greasy paper. This is a superb tale of forgiveness and freedom. She recognises Mrs Winterson's own depression and limitations.

The third is the ability to appreciate hot chips for what they are: that is, to draw nourishment even from a paltry emotional diet. For the young Winterson, this came through reading, an activity Mrs Winterson regarded as highly suspect. Once Jeanette got the bug, she hid books at home under her mattress until her bed started to rise higher and higher. When she found the books, Mrs Winterson burnt them, leaving fragments to flutter in the breeze around the yard. Winterson gathered some up some of the scorched pages and wonders if this is the source of her fragmentary style. She is an unencumbered reader. 'The library was my door to elsewhere,' she writes, and she springs through it. She relishes people such as T. S. Eliot who were strangers to her world. Her life was enriched by a long list of writers who have enriched my own: Anne Sexton, Melville (see Chapter 28) and Shakespeare (see Chapter 34). Perhaps we are more similar than I had thought. Indeed, when Winterson turns her attention to 'utility educators' whose interests are far too narrow, I want to raise a mug of tea in her honour.

CHAPTER 6

The Bottom of the Pile

Genelle Guzman-McMillan, *Angel in the Rubble* (2011)

Visit any bookstore and you may be surprised at how much memoir is on offer. Most of the time, there is more space devoted to autobiography than to biography. Perhaps this is further evidence of a narcissistic culture. Many of these memoirs have a short shelf life. They are formulaic and follow a predictable pattern. An eminent career does not always lead to an eminent book. An exciting sportsperson does not always produce an exciting memoir. These days, writing careers sometimes start where they used to end: with some kind of personal narrative. There is so much fiction in everyday life that readers are hungry for authenticity.

There are exceptions. *Angel in the Rubble* by Genelle Guzman-McMillan (born 1971) is not a great work of literature: it was produced with the help of a ghostwriter, William

Croyle. You may find it hard to locate a copy now. That's a pity. Like John Hersey's *Hiroshima* (1946) and Primo Levi's *If This Is a Man* (1947), it is an act of witness to one of the pivotal moments in the history of humanity's darkness. Genelle was the last person rescued alive from the wreckage of the Twin Towers in New York after the attacks of September 11, 2001. As she was stretchered from the ruins after a wait of twenty-seven hours, bystanders burst into applause. So did the people who were still glued to the TV, transfixed by anxiety. What was going to happen next?

I had the good fortune to spend an evening with Genelle Guzman-McMillan in 2011, a couple of weeks from the tenth anniversary of 9/11. It had been a disturbing year. Osama bin Laden was killed in May; Muammar Gaddafi was killed in October. My own mother had died in March; I was turning fifty. The world felt fragile. My sixteen-year-old students were telling me that the images from 9/11 were their earliest memories of anything outside their own families. They had grown up in a world of hostility.

For Genelle, that day started happily: it was a beautiful late summer's morning. She had moved to New York from Trinidad, had just patched up an argument with her boyfriend and was looking forward to her twelve-year-old daughter coming to join her in the United States. As she arrived for work on the sixty-fourth floor of the North Tower, she thought the sun was shining on her world. It didn't matter to her that she was five minutes late. She logged on at the Port Authority, the same organisation for which Herman Melville had once worked (see Chapter 28) and went in search of coffee.

Shortly afterwards, a plane hit the building. Genelle was probably one of the last people to understand what had happened. She and her colleagues waited a while, perhaps too long, before taking to the stairwell; they got as far as the thirteenth floor before the building fell on top of them. All the way down, Genelle held the hand of her friend Rosa Gonzalez. The pair had been planning a trip to Miami together. They were both single mums in promising new relationships. They both liked nightclubs. Genelle stopped to remove her shoes and lost Rosa's grip. That brief pause probably saved Genelle's life. Rosa was not so lucky.

Eventually a person called Paul took hold of Genelle's hand and held it for hour after hour, saying reassuring words. He was the angel in the rubble. 'As I held on to Paul, the pain throughout my body stopped.'

To the day we met, Genelle had never met Paul. Not waiting for thanks, he slipped away as she was freed.

Genelle, who is a quiet and modest woman, was slow to recognise her place at the heart of the catastrophe at the heart of the new century. Don DeLillo's novel about September 11, *Falling Man* (2007), begins with the line: 'It was not a street anymore but a world.'

Richard Dawkins has remarked that September 11 turned him into a radical atheist and, certainly, he has spent much of the time since trying to rid the world of religion. Genelle Guzman-McMillan has at least as much reason to be bitter about what happened. After all, her friends died, and she was left with a painful recovery involving many weeks in hospital and much rehabilitation. Yet, while nations went to war in retaliation, Genelle's own response was the discovery of peace. September 11 led her to think long and hard about nobody's beliefs but her own.

While she was buried under the rubble, something shifted in Genelle's guts. In the dark, unable to open her eyes, she turned to prayer, something she had not done for a long time. The prayer she discovered did not involve saying very much. On the contrary, it was a kind of listening. Genelle began to ponder all the ways in which her own life lacked peace. She resolved to change a number of things and to live less for herself. She had no way to know yet that the disaster she was caught up in had been meant to create terror. She rested in the words of a psalm her mother had taught her: 'Whom shall I fear?'

Genelle resolved that the only way she could respond to her situation, if she survived, was to try to live in a more loving way. Towards the end of the evening I spent with her, I asked Genelle how she felt when she heard that Osama bin Laden was killed, a couple of months earlier.

'I really don't know,' she said. 'I'm just grateful for life.'

CHAPTER 7

Riddikulus

J. K. Rowling, *Harry Potter and
the Prisoner of Azkaban* (1999)

I must have been the last person to join the Harry Potter
bandwagon. There was an occasion on which I was riding a
pushbike from Sydney to Melbourne because I was writing
a biography of the road that links Australia's two largest cities.
I use the word 'pushbike' advisedly: I spent just as much time
pushing as biking. For part of the trip I was on my own and on
one of those days I managed to find a room in an insalubrious
hotel in the Southern Highlands. There was plenty of noise
in the bar near my room but it made no difference. I slept like
the proverbial.

In the middle of the night, I woke and wondered where
I was. There were shadows on the walls around me and a
metal contraption pinning me to the bed. I realised this was
the pushbike. I pushed it off me and turned on my little radio.

Two pundits were discussing a wonderful new book for younger readers. They had clearly enjoyed *Harry Potter* but, being academics, were guarding their emotions with impregnable terms such as 'paradigm' and 'emotional demographics'. Anyway, it sounded like a book about a boarding school. Who would want to read that? I had worked in a boarding school. Apparently there was magic involved. Well, I had never seen much magic in the boarding school where I worked, although I had once walked in on a midnight séance in the Year 9 dormitory. The boys were trying to get in touch with the late Jimi Hendrix for some advice on the band they were forming.

I was sure such a silly book would have very limited appeal.

As so often, I had to eat my words. At least that's better than eating boarding-school food.

~

Before I knew it, my life was crowded with young people. Harry Potter became a welcome part of the time when our kids were little. We had Harry Potter parties and referred to ourselves as Muggles (the Potter word for ordinary humans) and spent a king's ransom on Harry Potter Lego, some of which, including the Knight Bus, now sits at the back of my teenage son's cupboard. For three years, I could rely on spending Christmas Day assembling the latest Lego megabox. I, too, grew up with Lego and counted the days until birthdays when another set would arrive. In those days, however, you had to figure out what to make with the pieces. I still have the little Lego motor I received for my tenth birthday. It could power trains and make lights shine; in its day, it was a true wonder. It is still in its box and, to my children, it is a curious antique.

We laughed about the idea of Muggle Quidditch and laughed again when we heard it was included as a demonstration sport at the London Olympics. I loved those days. They were, indeed, magic. When I started working at a large secondary school, my older son, Benedict, gave me a Lego figure of Dumbledore. My daughter, Clare, gave me one of Hagrid. Jacob, a boy of dreams, gave me a magic wand. Twelve years later, those three things are all still safely near my desk, although sometimes I wonder where the wild imagining behind the gifts has gone to hide. I hope one day it will return to free them from the dreariness of our Muggle muddle and soul-sapping computer games.

The Harry Potter stories were both innocent and sophisticated. For nights on end, when our three children shared the same room, Jenny would read from one of the steadily increasing number of books and the kids would urge her to keep going just for one more page, just till the end of the chapter. Sometimes Jenny could hardly stay awake but the kids, who'd been desperate for sleep an hour before, would be now wide-eyed, dreading the moment when it was time for prayers and the land of nod.

Above all, I can remember a car trip from our former home back to Melbourne, a distance of more than six hundred kilometres. We were not looking forward to the journey as the kids were grumpy travellers but we had Stephen Fry on CD reading *Harry Potter and the Prisoner of Azkaban*, the third book in the series and possibly my favourite.

My life has been wonderfully enriched by talking books: I love being read to. If I have to face a mountain of ironing on a Sunday afternoon, I will actually relish the task if I have an unabridged recording of something vast by Dickens on my iPod. I will take the long way home in the car to have a few more paragraphs of *Jane Eyre* (see Chapter 29) or lines of *The Canterbury Tales* (see Chapter 35). When I went to Africa with a group of young people, I uploaded *War and Peace* (see Chapter 26). It not only helped kill the time on long flights, especially when, travelling on the cheapest ticket, I was squashed in the middle seat, but there were times when the book helped me get a bit of distance from some of the pain we encountered in the poverty of Kenya and Tanzania. Talking books are a great way to rediscover a book you thought you knew: the reader will cast an entirely new light on familiar words.

I will never forget the last four hundred and fifty kilometres of our journey home with *Harry Potter and the Prisoner of Azkaban*. The whole way, the kids did not want to stop for the toilet. They did not even want to stop for junk food.

When we finally reached our house, they all remained in the car until the end of the disc we were on. They had been utterly transfixed. By now, I was thoroughly jealous of the author.

I was slowly being won over to the idea of Harry Potter as Literature. I was a diehard Tolkien fan and admired the way his sentences unfurled into the middle distance. J. K. Rowling's sentences are more likely to have a scarcely perceptible smile playing about them. I was fascinated by the Tolkien story, of a musty gentleman in love with language. His translation of the Book of Jonah in *The Jerusalem Bible* is joyous and wise.

He was an academic who volunteered as a signaller for the 11th Lancashire Fusiliers and was behind the lines on the first day of the Somme in July 1916. The weeks he spent in the inhuman catastrophe of the Western Front were the seedbed for an extraordinary epic about the contest between havoc and order, destruction and hope. He was lucky to have suffered trench fever and have been sent back to England.

He was unwell for the next three years but during that time he invented a number of Elvish languages, such as Quenya and Sindarin. It was a time in which others began to lose confidence in what language might do. The philosopher Ludwig Wittgenstein was among their leading lights. But Tolkien rowed against the cultural tide and from his faith in language came faith in a huge narrative that might explain life in all its complexity.

Rowling (born 1965) is also a writer of courageous vision. At the time she was working on *Harry Potter and the Philosopher's Stone*, the first book of the series, she was a single mother. Her marriage had broken up and her bank account was notably lacking in Galleons. Her mother died of multiple sclerosis as Rowling was writing. She suffered depression and a sense of disorientation. Nobody wanted to publish her book. I imagine that the daily grind was plenty for her to contend with. Yet she created a narrative that, like Tolkien's, embraces an understanding of the whole of life, not just her corner of it. All the incidents of the stories fall under an overarching sense of right and wrong, and the significance of moral choices. There is a central character, Voldemort, who embodies evil. He is known as the one whose name may not be spoken.

Rowling is drawing upon centuries of human grappling with the elusive banality of evil (see Chapter 14).

The Harry Potter books are part of a tradition of writing for younger readers in which teenagers are separated from parental protection and constraint: they must assume responsibility for their world much sooner than they might otherwise be expected to do so. Robert Muchamore's Cherub series, John Marsden's Tomorrow series and even C. S. Lewis's *The Lion, the Witch and the Wardrobe* are just a few examples.

Hogwarts, the school at the heart of the Harry Potter world, also has a rich understanding of the nature of education. Adults, with all their flaws, have a crucial role. Teaching there is both experiential and theoretical. It includes plenty of material with an ancient pedigree. It honours arcane traditions which require humility and perseverance to master. Everyone knows that what they are doing is really important; there is a complex relationship between teachers and their subject matter. You could create an entire course in education out of the approach to teaching of a list of characters that work at Hogwarts.

I've often wondered what school was like for J. K. Rowling. The series tends to focus as much on teaching as learning. Education happens in the context of a relationship. It is not about downloading material from a website and submitting assessment online. At Hogwarts, the students are treated with warmth, affection and respect. They are also significantly challenged. But the world and the expectations of their learning is not simply built around them. They are being led into the wisdom of their ancestors. It is a fantastic model of education.

One of the proudest moments of my career was when some of my students started referring to me as Dumbledore. I didn't deserve the honour and the nickname didn't stick for long.

There is wisdom and satire in *Harry Potter and the Prisoner of Azkaban*. Ron Weasley's inability to cope with a phone (which he calls a 'fellytone', prompting Hermione to urge him to take 'Muggles studies next year') leads him to resort to owl post, with which he is more comfortable. The story includes Boggarts, beings that present themselves in the form of your worst fear. Professor Lupin, who teaches 'defence against the dark arts', explains that 'the thing that really finished a Boggart is laughter.' You imagine your fear in some hilarious outfit and then, with 'force of mind', say the spell to get rid of them, which is the word 'riddikulus'. The idea of getting young readers, not to mention older ones, to mock their fears is terrific. So too is Professor Lupin's advice in dealing with Dementors. A Dementor resembles a kind of mental illness, such as depression: 'They infest the darkest, filthiest places, they glory in decay and despair, they drain peace, hope and happiness out of the air around them…Get too near a Dementor and every good feeling, every happy memory will be sucked out of you.'

The prison in this world, Azkaban, has no walls because prisoners are 'all trapped inside their own heads, incapable of a single cheerful thought'.

We all need to learn skills in dealing with the Dementors in our lives. The world of Hogwarts may be invented, but it is not escapist.

~

When Benedict, my son, was thirteen and starting his second year of high school, we were invited to a 'father and son evening' where everybody was asked to bring an object they treasured and which they could chat about with each other, invoking the very happy memories that Dementors can't stand. I brought some photos. Benedict brought a paperback copy of *Harry Potter and the Chamber of Secrets* that we had walked up to the local bookshop together to buy on a sunny Sunday afternoon, six and a half years earlier. I had written in the book for him. It took us back to a time when I was still 'daddy' rather than 'dad' and our fears seemed ridiculous.

CHAPTER 8

Because There Is Pain

Annie Proulx, *Close Range* (1999)

Annie Proulx (born 1935) can seem like a formidable figure. My aunt Nona didn't have this problem. Nona had the incisive kind of mind that could sharpen itself on the whetstone of Proulx's granite prose. Proulx is one of those writers who knows how to hold her silence. She didn't publish her first book until she was fifty-six. She lived life the right way round. A lot of people do their talking young and learn to listen later.

Nona read books like her life depended on it. She could talk and listen simultaneously. Her fluency was famous. One time, she left the table to answer the phone, leaving the rest of us to think that we wouldn't see her again for quite some time. Nevertheless, she returned to us after a mere twenty minutes.

'That was a quick call,' someone said.

'It was a wrong number,' she replied, without apology, before leaning in to complete the sentence she had left unfinished. Her conversation was torrential; it made things grow.

Nona took exception to *The Shipping News* (1993), Proulx's Pulitzer Prize-winning second novel, because she found it so bleak. A newspaperman called Quoyle moves from New York to allow his life to be reshaped by the forces of nature in Newfoundland. In the early pages, both Quoyle's parents die in awful circumstances and he discovers his wife is making extra cash as a sex worker. She then dies in a car crash and Quoyle is left with their two kids to look after. By the time Nona read this fiction, she had already buried two of her own children, one as a baby and the other as a young adult. One death was foreseen, the other not, but foresight does nothing to soften the colours of grief. Nona spoke of many things but not this. Except to Annie Proulx, when about five hundred other people were listening in. Hers was the first hand in the air at a literary event we both attended.

'Two of my children have died,' said Nona. 'Why do I need to read books like yours when I have enough reality of my own?'

The audience applauded the question.

Proulx was stunned and consulted with the chairwoman who was on the stage with her.

'I am sorry for your pain,' she said. 'But that is why I write. I write because there *is* pain, not to make pain.'

The audience applauded the answer.

Annie Proulx is a tough writer. There are times when reading her stories feels like washing your face with sandpaper.

For all that, or because of it, *Close Range* is an extraordinary collection of stories, far more exacting than *The Shipping News*. They use very little emotional language to describe the profound emotional struggles of isolated people. *Close Range* is an uncomfortable source of comfort.

The book includes 'Brokeback Mountain', which was made into a movie by Ang Lee. It is one of the most masterly stories I have ever encountered, and it is a pity that both it and the movie carry the burden of being typecast as 'the gay cowboy story'. 'Brokeback Mountain' is not about homosexuality but the suffocation of it. It sorrows for the ways in which fear curdles tenderness, turns it sour. The heart of the story is not a relationship but loneliness and isolation. Like many of the stories in this great book, it scorns the idea of an individual trying to dominate or control their world. 'Brokeback Mountain' ends with a flinty statement of fatalism without grace or redemption: 'There was some open space between what he knew and what he tried to believe, but nothing could be done about it, and if you can't fix it you've got to stand it.'

All the stories in *Close Range* are set in Wyoming, where Proulx moved in the mid-1990s. Wyoming is the least populous state of the United States and large parts of it, especially in the west, are inhabited by rock. It is also 93 per cent white and less than 2 per cent African American. It is not wealthy. There are as many guns as people, probably more. Clichés abound to describe such people and 'trailer trash' might be one of them, but Annie Proulx is not much interested in clichés.

There is a minor character in one of these stories, 'The Governors of Wyoming', called Skipper. For once, cattle prices

are solid and he pays cash for a car for his wife. Their two sons
are mucking around and manage to get trapped in the trunk
of dad's new trophy:

> Out there on the prairie something—the evasive turn of
> a harried bird with a motion like a convulsive kick?—
> made him stop and open the trunk. In that airless oven
> they lay limp and blue. It was wrong what they said
> about grief. It augered inside you forever, boring fresh
> holes even when you were sieved. Ziona lived now in
> San Diego, remarried, and with other children, but he
> was still here seeing the places they had been every day.

These few lines bear the scorch marks of Proulx's genius.
Nature is an implacable God. The inevitable collapse of a
marriage happens in the space between two sentences. Above
all, there is a withering insight into the nature of grief.

~

There is abundant humour in Proulx. We meet a rodeo rider
who believes Jesus was a cowboy because the Bible says Jesus
rode bareback on an unbroken donkey. This man becomes
a wisdom figure. There is another man who gets killed by
an emu because someone thinks they can make a buck out
of bringing Australian fauna into the ranch country. There
is, in 'Job History', an understanding of the way life can be
so intense that it denies life. There are few lucky breaks. You
sense that Annie Proulx longs for things to be different but she
isn't prepared to lie just to make it so.

CHAPTER 9

Long Time Shaving

Nelson Mandela, *Long Walk to Freedom* (1994)

Long Walk to Freedom by Nelson Mandela (1918–2013) was supposed never to be written. By the mid-1970s, when Mandela had been imprisoned on Robben Island for more than a decade, the world had not heard a word from him for years. The South African press was banned from publishing his photo or quoting anything he had ever said. He had been refused permission even to attend the funeral of his eldest son. Mandela, along with those who shared his imprisonment, posed a risk to the apartheid regime which excluded blacks, who comprised the majority of the South African population, not just from power but from practically every human right.

After a time, conditions for Mandela and his comrades improved slightly. Some were even allowed to study. This meant they had access to paper. Mandela began secretly to compose a memoir of grace and wisdom. The handwritten drafts had to be buried in the prison's vegetable patch. Had they been discovered, the consequences for producing something of such beauty and truth would have been dire.

I grew up in a world where it seemed that every fence and every hoarding carried a sign that said 'Free Nelson Mandela'. Now the signs all say 'Free Wi-Fi'. Apartheid was the soundtrack of my teenage years. It had a major effect on sport and so many bands performed songs on the topic. Everyone from U2 and Simple Minds to Stevie Wonder sang about it. Peter Gabriel released a song in 1980 called 'Biko', about Steve Biko, the founder of the black-consciousness movement which led to the Soweto uprisings of 1976 and a resurgence of protest, focussed in particular on an absurd education policy. Gabriel's song said that you could blow out a candle but not a fire. There was a lot of noise on the subject. Everyone at a safe distance protested on the top of their lungs. Those closest to the lived reality, though, spent a lot of time in silence.

In 2014, I was with a group of young people who went to Africa as part of Zimele, a community whose name was borrowed from Steve Biko. Zimele was established to try to build bridges between the privileged world in which my students and I live and the world in which most people on earth live. We visited the Apartheid Museum in Soweto which, as its name implies, began as a township southwest of Johannesburg. The museum was paid for by gambling money, principally revenue raised in taxes from the garish casino nearby where people of any colour are welcome to come and lose their money. Plenty of other cultural entities around the world, such as movies and galleries, have been made possible from gaming revenue—almost as if the governments that are so reliant on this source of income want to throw a few shekels back to the public as guilt money. But none of that need undermine the quiet, dignified and candid manner in which the Apartheid Museum tells its horrendous story.

On a Saturday morning, there was hardly anyone else there. There were exhibits that nailed me to the ground. One was of a massive yellow Casspir, the infamous vehicle that was developed in South Africa for subduing the black population in townships. It was a fort on wheels that could carry fourteen troops and was able to resist mine explosions. The improvised shantytowns were no match for it. It could push them over like cardboard. Even in the safety of a museum, I felt a frisson of fear as it towered over me.

There was also the famous recording of Nelson Mandela speaking at the trial for sabotage at which he was finally condemned to life imprisonment, in 1964. The sound is grainy but Mandela's voice is slow and deliberate. This is a man on trial for his life. He plants every word:

> I have cherished the ideal of a democratic and free society in which all persons live together in harmony and with equal opportunities. It is an ideal which I hope to live for and to achieve. But if needs be, it is an ideal for which I am prepared to die.

This speech has been replicated many times. At the museum, you can buy T-shirts and mugs with those words on them. On that occasion, his last public appearance for twenty-six years, Mandela spoke for four hours. He was not going to be rushed. Then he disappeared from public view until 11 February 1990. On that day, I was sitting in the early hours of the morning watching a TV in Melbourne with two young Jesuits from South Africa as Mandela was released from custody. Both of them were crying. When Mandela finally appeared, holding the hand of his then wife, Winnie, it was not the man I expected to see. My mind still carried the image of the posters that plastered the billboards of my youth: a much younger and physically impressive man, one you wouldn't want to mess with. I felt at once that this new Mandela was bigger than revenge. You could see it in the careful way he walked.

At the Apartheid Museum, I spent fifteen minutes watching a video of Mandela shaving. The film draws the onlooker into a richer and more mysterious intimacy with him than any amount of footage of his numerous appearances. As president of South Africa, Mandela maintained many of the quiet rituals that had enabled him to survive his decades in prison. He made his own bed, following an inflexible pattern. He did his exercise beside his bed, even though the president would surely have had access to a gym, because that was a ritual that sustained him. His handwriting was fastidious. For both good and ill, the president was still the prisoner.

Watching him, I began to think about my own frenetic approach to shaving. I often shaved under the shower to save time. It was a job to be got out of the way so I could move on to other frenetic activities. Yet I was a schoolteacher. Mandela was running a country and really had stuff to worry about.

His shaving was a meditation, a sign of freedom. I hoped that I might find a less anxious way of living, or at least of shaving.

As we were having a cup of coffee, John Mount, a fellow teacher, said that he could recall a time in the early 1960s when he was glad that Mandela was in jail because he thought that Mandela and the African National Congress were all communists. He laughs at himself now, but apartheid would have fallen apart much sooner except that the Reagan and Thatcher administrations, in the United States and Britain respectively, hid behind a fear of communism.

I mentioned to Tom Purcell, the founder of Zimele and leader of our group, that I had a kind of envy of Mandela and those who shared the journey with him because they had such a strong sense of what their purpose was in life.

Tom reacted against this. 'But at what cost,' he said. 'Mandela had three marriages. He was unable to attend the funeral of his oldest son. He said in his mid-eighties that he was supposed to be the grandfather of the nation when he didn't even know his own children.'

Even the 2005 death of his son Makgatho, at the age of fifty-four as a result of AIDS, was a public matter. AIDS was a huge issue in South Africa and Mandela has been criticised for his tardiness in addressing it. He made an announcement: 'Let us give publicity to HIV/AIDS and not hide it because that is the only way to make it appear like a normal illness.'

Aged eighty, Mandela married Graça Machel, the widow of Samora Machel, the former president of Mozambique. 'We were both very, very lonely,' she said as millions looked on.

In *Long Walk to Freedom*, Mandela writes about the manner in which his political commitments had prevented him from helping his mother:

> Her difficulties, her poverty, made me question once again whether I had taken the right path. That was always the conundrum: Had I made the right choice in putting the people's welfare even before that of my own family?

~

One of my favourite parts of *Long Walk to Freedom* concerns a period in the course of his long captivity when Mandela was at last allowed to have a small garden. For years he had been refused this permission without being given any reason. Then, still without reason, the system changed its mind.

> A garden was one of the few things in prison that one could control. To plant a seed, watch it grow, to tend it and then harvest it offered a simple but enduring satisfaction. The sense of being the custodian of this small patch of earth offered a small taste of freedom.

CHAPTER 10

Finding Centre

Thea Astley, *Reaching Tin River* (1990)

I used to think that Thea Astley (1925–2004) was in every way the opposite of her older brother, Phillip, with whom I lived for six memorable years. But then she showed me the room in which she did her writing. It was not like the rest of her house.

~

In my twenties, I was part of a small group of Jesuits who, on our holidays, used to visit Thea and her husband, Jack, in their home high on the range that overlooked the Shoalhaven River, a few hours south of Sydney by car. Thea loved the audience. Jack sat quietly to one side, smoking, while Thea occupied centre stage, also smoking. She was witty and sarcastic, and her voice could cut through leather. For ages, she would hold forth, asking the most intimate questions in a demanding voice then saying, 'You don't have to answer that,' then answering the question herself. It was great fun. Jack was never required to say much.

The only thing Thea didn't allow us to ask about was her own work, a topic that was strictly off limits. She was brazen about many things but reserved about the inner life of her novels. One time, I was poking around among the old books on the shelves of the Catholic parish in Toowong, an inner suburb of Brisbane. I stumbled across a copy of Thea Astley's first novel, *Girl with a Monkey*, published in 1958 when Thea was thirty-three. Like many debut novels, it draws on Astley's personal experience, especially as a schoolteacher in regional Queensland, a stifling existence from which she had been desperate to escape. Astley's extraordinary career spanned more than forty years and teachers often surface in her novels, nearly always as people who have been excluded from the life they really want to be living. Astley began writing partly to free herself from the arid existence of the classroom. *Girl with a Monkey* was completed while her only child was a baby.

The copy I had come across was not just any copy. It was the one she had inscribed and dedicated to her parents: Cecil and Eileen, an odd couple. Bear in mind that Astley won Australia's most prestigious writing prize, the Miles Franklin Literary Award, on no fewer than four occasions; nobody has won it more often. Astley blazed a trail for all writers but especially for women: she was gifted at describing the invisible prisons in which people get locked up. So the book I had in my hands had a significant place in Australian cultural history. I returned it to her with a mild query about it ending up in such a strange place.

'I have no idea how it got there,' replied Thea.

It was difficult to get past that guard.

Thea was far more kind than she wanted people to know. But she pretended she couldn't remember much about her books, although she could quote reviews, especially bad ones, by heart. I can't remember a meeting with her over the years of our friendship in which she didn't mention that Patrick White, Australia's Nobel laureate and, I think, her unspoken rival, had said to somebody or other that Thea told a decent story. I am not sure if she was pleased or displeased by such paltry praise. She did, however, want to know that we had read her books and when one of us, Ed, confessed that he had not, she was unimpressed in a self-mocking kind of way.

'What are the books like?' asked Ed on the way home.

They are as sharp and trenchant and cutting as she was. But they are also wise, compassionate and lean. Not a wasted word. Thea once told me that she treated her stories like anchovy paste. She spread them as much as possible to cover every corner of the toast. This is the kind of pasty metaphor that she would never have tolerated in her own novels but she meant that she didn't waste material.

~

Phillip, Thea's only sibling, was quietly spoken and so gentle it was sometimes difficult even to feel his presence in a room. In the Jesuit world of big personalities, he demanded very little. But he had hands made of steel and could peel an orange faster than anyone else in history, tearing at the rind and then the pith as if the fruit needed to be punished. We lived together in a community and, much as I enjoyed and admired Thea,

I came to love Phillip. I have been close to only two saints and he was one of them. He was extremely modest, entering a shower cubicle fully clothed and emerging the same way.

Like Thea, Phillip was no stranger to mental anguish and his suffering had brought him to a kind of mellowness that, as a self-important young windbag, I did not understand. His life had not been easy. He had been sent to teach primary-school children, who ate him alive. Indeed, at his funeral in 1997, one of the priests introduced himself to Thea and started regaling her with funny stories about what a disaster he had been in the classroom.

'Well, father,' she said in a voice that could have made the statues blush, 'at least he did his best.'

Later, he went to England to pursue a calling to the contemplative life at Ampleforth Abbey as a Benedictine monk, an order with a wonderful ability to combine beauty and asceticism. Things didn't work out and, returning to Australia, he was not sure where he fitted in. He fell into a deep hole and, I believe, hardly said a word for five years, not even, I suspect, to God. On several occasions, he was hospitalised for poor mental health. A friend wrote: 'He had lost confidence in himself; he had lost his sense of belonging.' This was the dark night of his soul.

Phillip came back to life thanks to friendship and faith, the two areas in which he found love. That is a long and beautiful story. Music played a big part in it. On cold winter afternoons, you could hear him playing the organ on his own in the chapel. Often, when he played, he took off his fine-rimmed spectacles and turned off his hearing aid. He was entering his cave to see if God had left him any morsel. He was a braver man than I ever could be.

There are many priests in Thea's novels. Most of them are portraits of cruelty and complacency, with the possible exception of Father Dempsey in *The Multiple Effects of Rainshadow* (1996). None of her priests are the least bit like Phillip. Yet the room in which she wrote was very much like a room in which you could imagine Phillip finding peace. There was a piano against the wall. On a small table there was a typewriter. That was it. It was bare and ascetic but, if you knew Thea, it had everything you needed to make something beautiful out of all the petty antagonisms of life. Her two keyboards were closely related.

~

As he was dying, Phillip leaned back on his pillow at the hospice and looked at the ceiling.

'I am a homosexual,' he said loudly. It was strange to hear this quiet man yelling. He sounded like he was ready to rip the skin off an orange. He didn't care who heard: he was free.

~

Phillip was lightened by innocence; Thea was burdened by guilt.

After Phillip's funeral, Thea asked if I could take her to see Helen Daniel, then the editor of *Australian Book Review*. Helen's partner had just died and Thea wanted to extend her sympathy in person. Yet the first thing she said to Helen when we arrived unannounced at the office was: 'You feel like you did it, don't you?'

Helen was also a colossal smoker. She used to run a second-hand bookshop where she sat behind the counter with a book in one hand and a cigarette in the other. They were both on their second cigarette by the time Helen could find an answer.

'Yes,' she said.

Later, Helen told how much she'd been helped in that moment by Thea's dark candour. Thea seemed to be implying that however much Helen had looked after her partner, she would still feel inadequate. This was the closest I saw Thea to sharing Phillip's understanding of the dark night. But Thea's language tended to be one of guilt: *You feel like you did it.*

In our last conversation, Thea told me that she had been a terrible wife, a terrible mother, a terrible person. None of this was true.

'But you have been a terrible pessimist,' I said.

~

Of all Thea's books, I keep returning to *Reaching Tin River*, a work of beauty and depth set mostly in Astley's heartland of regional Queensland. It is less autobiographical than works such as *It's Raining in Mango* (1987), which deal with the history of Astley's forebears. But the journey of the central character, Belle, is one in which Astley shows her own heart more than anywhere else. The result is both poignant and witheringly funny. Belle is the result of a brief marriage between her mother, Bonnie, a drummer, and Huck, a trumpet player who returns to America. Later, tired of life as a teacher and then a librarian, Belle will go to America looking for Huck, a journey that takes her to a trailer park in search of faint clues. She marries Seb, a cruel and callous individual. Little by little, Belle sheds the uniform she has been expected to wear, in order to pursue a vision of her own. Again and again, she says she is looking for a centre, toying with images from Euclid to make light of the untidy geometry of life. This phrase is a refrain throughout the story: it occurs on many occasions in numerous guises. The blind and gutsy search for a centre is what the dark night of the soul is all about.

Thea and Phillip both worked hard on the task.

CHAPTER 11

The Other Side of the River

Toni Morrison, *Beloved* (1987)

Toni Morrison (born 1931) has spent fifty years drawing poison from the wounds of black America. She has written as the heiress of a heavy fortune, the suffering of her family and people, and she has invested that fortune in a profound search for truth, wisdom and healing. She is one of the few writers who have reduced me to tears. That's not quite right. She has elevated me to tears.

Toni Morrison can use tears to break a drought. In a recent novel, *God Help the Child* (2015), written when the Nobel laureate was in her eighties, she shows, as she always has, an uncanny ability to feel the pain of children and see through their eyes. One of those children is Bride, now a successful black businesswoman working in the fashion industry. Bride is drawn with exquisite sensuality: Toni Morrison describes sex with shades of every colour. In *Home* (2012), one character, Cee, finds of sex that 'it was not so much painful as dull… its pleasure lay in its brevity.' The first phrase of her first book, *The Bluest Eye* (1970), is 'Nuns go by as quiet as lust', truly an image for the ages. Bride, on the other hand, finds that sex with the damaged Booker is a three-course meal, a banquet of raucous feeling that leaves her so replete that it staves off emotion from her own damaged childhood.

Bride, whose real name is Lula Ann Bridewell, is the black child of a woman, Sweetness, with much paler skin. Bride's colour is a genetic conundrum and Morrison uses it to explore gradations of prejudice based on shades of black. Sweetness finds her child unbearable to embrace and Bride, like so many of Morrison's young characters, suffers the consequences of a childhood without affectionate touch. She becomes so desperate that she is prepared to lie in a court case when she is eight just to get a hug from her mother. Her lies sent Sofia Huxley to jail for fifteen years on charges of sexual abuse. Bride feels so guilty (guilt is another vein which Morrison mines) that she waits for Sofia's release from jail, follows her to a motel, and tries to give her a bag of luxury personal items and a five-thousand-dollar travel voucher. Sofia reacts violently and brutally attacks Bride. Later, Sofia considers that Bride has done her a favour: 'the release of tears unshed for fifteen years. No more bottling up. No more filth. Now I am clean and able.'

The poet Paul Muldoon has said of Morrison that 'in her novels the pressure per square inch is very high.' This is especially true of her masterpiece *Beloved*, which I discovered in a general store in regional Queensland in 1989 where, two

years after publication, it had been remaindered along with the
year's calendars and diaries. God knows how it had found its
way into an area that was not itself especially well known for
sympathetic relationships between black and white citizens,
but there it was for eight dollars in a hefty hardcover. I had
no idea what I was buying; I just knew that I didn't feel like
reading an empty diary.

At the time, I was a young teacher and had been press-
ganged by the headmaster of the boarding school where I was
working into spending the term break helping to take a group
of teenagers on a bus trip from Sydney to the Great Barrier
Reef. I had made the mistake of telling him that I was hoping
to spend the break reading. This man was so bossy that they
eventually made him a bishop. In *Beloved*, Morrison describes
someone as 'a deeply religious man who knew what God
knew and told everybody what it was'. She must have worked
for the same guy.

To be fair, this principal was good at his job and did me
the kind of favours that one resents at first. In my first year,
I was struggling to bring order to the bedlam of the teenage
classroom. The racket in my classes could be heard from here
to kingdom come, a destination that was not coming fast.
I reacted by preparing lots of reading material and worksheets,
thinking I could bury my problem under a blanket of paper.
One Sunday afternoon, I was in at school getting things ready
for the next day. The photocopier was running hot outside
the principal's office and, in the middle of the afternoon, he
appeared at my side.

'What are you doing?'

I was pleased that I'd be getting kudos for working on a Sunday. 'I'm getting my classes ready.'

He looked at the mountain of material I had already duplicated and then slipped away into his office. About half an hour later he appeared again. The mountain had grown even higher.

'Is this for the whole semester?' he asked, incredulous.

'No, this is just for tomorrow.'

'Tomorrow!'

I caught the bemusement in his tone. 'And the next day.'

He grumbled a kind of laugh. He was not unkind. 'Just remember one thing,' he said.

'What's that?'

'Just remember that you are paid to talk to kids.'

I haven't forgotten his pithy summary of teaching, especially as education has followed my early mistakes and turned them into virtues, filling every space in every diary, sometimes with rubble more than substance.

The principal thought I'd be better off on a bus trip of several thousand kilometres and he was right. Along the way, as we visited Fraser Island, we had the whole group packed into the back of a four-wheel-drive people mover that was open to the air. The driver, who was white and middle-aged, made as if to run down a beach fisherman, who was black and middle-aged. The fisherman made a rude gesture, entirely justified in the circumstances. The driver hit the brakes, jumped out and began a brawl with the beach fisherman, ending up with a bloodied nose and possibly a cracked rib as well. Our students never forgot it. It was worth all the theory about black and white Australia in the world. A black man had dared to protest against a truck tearing up his beach and almost running him down.

That night, I picked up this vast tapestry of a book called *Beloved*. It was about a dead baby whose mother, a former slave, could not afford the money to put 'Dearly beloved' on a tombstone. She could only stretch herself to the word 'Beloved', so that is what the dear departed came to be known as; Morrison has said that her characters tell her their names and if she gets the wrong name, nothing happens. A lot happens with Beloved because in this case the departed has not left but mysteriously hangs around: this is the hook from which the story hangs. As I sat in a cabin reading by the light of a torch, it choked me up. As Muldoon implies, the book puts pressure on every bruise and sore spot you have acquired along the way.

The following day, I was talking with the kids about the incident of the day before. They all had opinions. I couldn't get a word in. But listening is the most active part of conversation, the part at which I am not very good. A fifteen-year-old kid spoke about the death of his dog that had been hit by a car. The boy had cried for days, much to the annoyance of his father. The father sounded remote. I wondered if he might even have been jealous of the dog. Dogs never say the wrong thing. We had a great talk. Within four years, that boy had died in a car accident as well. Toni Morrison knows all about such fragility: in her world, lives may end but the pain endures.

~

Morrison was born in Ohio, a place she has explored in breadth and depth. Her wry affection for the landscape is evident in *Beloved*: 'In Ohio seasons are theatrical. Each one enters like a prima donna, convinced its performance is the reason the world has people in it.' In that book, the Ohio River is the border that escaping slaves need to negotiate. Freedom, whatever that might mean, lies on the other side of the river. One character puts the experience into words. 'My heart's beating,' she says.

Morrison's family moved around a great deal, always finding it hard to pay the rent. Her dad worked three jobs. Her grandparents were Southerners with memories of a time when it was illegal to teach black people to read and write because providing those skills was such a risk. So Morrison, who was Chloe Wofford when she went to school, prized education and the freedom it created.

Before long, Morrison was partnered and had two sons and, before much longer again, she was a single mother with two sons. She found a career as an editor in publishing and was the midwife for some remarkable books that gave voice to black experience, not least by Muhammad Ali and Angela Davis. She was nothing if not busy and coped by writing lists. She says there was a point in her life at which she stopped writing lists of what she had to do and started writing lists of what she wanted to do.

She found only two items of importance on the new list. She wanted to be able to mother her children. And she wanted to write books of her own. Being a mother has meant accompanying one of her sons, an artist, on his difficult journey through cancer to death. She now lives and works surrounded by his paintings. Becoming a writer started with the notebooks that were always by her side, whether in the car or at home or anywhere. She gathered snippets from every corner of her world.

Her debut novel, *The Bluest Eye*, took five years to write and did not receive much attention. Like *God Help the Child* and many of her works, it deals with self-rejection, a soul-destroying skill that has to be taught by others. In this case, Morrison recalls the story of a beautiful girl who was in her class in elementary school. The girl said that she had definite proof that God could not exist. The proof was that she had been praying for two years to have blue eyes and God had not answered her request. This was a turning point for Morrison. She knew at once that it would have been a tragedy if God had changed the girl's eyes. The sorrow was that she could not see her own beauty. In the novel, she becomes the victim of incest and falls pregnant to her father, a man who has also been schooled to reject any beauty in himself.

Beloved began its life from a small cutting Morrison found in a paper concerning Margaret Garner, who escaped from slavery in Kentucky but then faced recapture. Rather than allow her baby to become the property of someone else, she kills it. In the novel, this character, Sethe, uses a handsaw for her dire purpose. She experiences rejection from the whole community and for twelve years nobody visits her house, which becomes possessed by the ghost of the child. Morrison tells this story in all its dreadful complexity. *Beloved* is a work whose sustained moral stamina strengthens us, her readers, to confront horror ourselves. In an essay in *Burn this Book* (2009), Morrison writes:

I have been told that there are two human responses to the perception of chaos: naming and violence...Certain kinds of trauma visited on peoples are so deep, so cruel, that unlike money, unlike vengeance, even unlike justice, or rights, or the goodwill of others, only writers can translate such trauma and turn sorrow into meaning, sharpening the moral imagination.

CHAPTER 12

Large

Les Murray, 'An Absolutely
Ordinary Rainbow' (1969)

The Australian poet Les Murray (born 1938) is larger than life. There have been people who have wanted to cut him down to size, but that's easier said than done. Murray doesn't shape his cloth to suit the latest fashion. He is sceptical of hype. He is physically large and a little gauche in an age in which people are easily embarrassed by anything that doesn't fit a narrow mould.

Les Murray has been acclaimed as a possible Nobel laureate and derided as a political intransigent. Yet his work is beyond such easy headlines. I prefer the man whose wit can nail the human ego to the floor as he does in a three-line poem, 'Senryu', from early in his career:

Just two hours after
Eternal Life pills came out
Someone took thirty.

Half a century later, in 'Diabetica', he can turn the ungodly phenomenon of a man getting up in the night to piss into an almost mystical quest:

A man coughs like a box
and turns on yellow light
to follow his bladder

out over the gunwale
of his bed.

My first encounter with Murray, if you can call it that, was when I was at university. It was advertised that the poet, who has spent most of his life around the tiny settlement of Bunyah on the north coast of New South Wales, was coming to the big smoke and would read his poetry. I was excited. 'An Absolutely Ordinary Rainbow' was absolutely my favourite poem at the time. I had found it in Murray's first collection, *The Weatherboard Cathedral* (1969), whose title appealed to me instantly because of the way it brought together two architectural extremes: the mighty and the modest.

Murray arrived in the English Department in a boilermaker's suit and sat on a table. He bent his book back at the spine until it cracked. He twisted around as though his own spine had cracked. Then he began with 'The Quality of Sprawl', a poem whose vision of unconventional largesse is infectious:

Sprawl is the quality
of the man who cut his Rolls-Royce
into a farm utility truck, and sprawl
is what the company lacked when it made repeated efforts
to buy the vehicle back and repair its image.

In my callow judgement, Murray's reading was dreadful. It was like hearing Bob Dylan grating through his 'Blowin' in the Wind' once you've heard Peter, Paul and Mary present the sweet version. Murray was too fast. He mumbled. He didn't look at us or engage us. He didn't pause at the end of one poem before he rushed into the next one. He didn't show any recognition that part of what he was reading was extremely funny; part of it was desperately poignant. There was no element of performance in it at all.

This was precisely the point. Murray's poetry is brilliant because both he and it are lacking in arrogance. His poetry listens: it has an astonishing ear for the most delicate cadences of language. Murray is a servant of that language, not its proprietor.

Years later, Murray found something I had written in a little magazine he had picked up in church. He rang me up because he wanted to discuss it. I was working as a Jesuit priest at the time but, even so, I was not above being flattered by attention from a personal hero. He also wanted to talk about the opening ceremony of the 2000 Sydney Olympics, which was coming up. There was a fair bit of hype surrounding the event. I, like many, was looking forward to it. I knew people who had taken part in the torch relay that went past the door of the bluestone church beside which I was living; the local school-crossing attendant had brought traffic to a standstill for ten minutes so it could go through. I don't mind a bit of community colour and I still chuckle when I think of Rowan Atkinson's send-up of *Chariots of Fire* at the opening ceremony of the 2012 London Olympics. But Les had other concerns. He told me that the whole idea of the opening ceremony, as we now know it, was the brainchild of Joseph Goebbels and that we wouldn't have it except for the travesty of the Berlin games of 1936. He didn't quite say that Sydney was about to stage its own version of a Nuremberg Rally. Nor was he showing any undue enthusiasm. He told me that Hugo Boss had supplied the uniforms for the Third Reich. It was hard to imagine Les Murray wearing Hugo Boss anyway.

I told him that the only Olympic event in which I could compete would be the small bore. He laughed.

When I left the Jesuit order, Les was vexed and sent me an unpoetic fax to express his disappointment on behalf of ordinary parishioners who needed people to stick by them. I explained the reasons behind my change of life and he sent me a beautiful apology. Les understood pain. 'An Absolutely Ordinary Rainbow' is one of countless places where he expresses that pain. I think that is why it spoke to me in my late adolescence and continues to do so.

The poem begins with the line: 'The word goes round Repins'. This barked at me. Repins was a coffee shop in King Street, Sydney, established in the 1930s by a Russian refugee. It was famous during the Depression for the number of struggling salesmen, working on commission, who would huddle inside to do their paperwork. It was also the place where a generation of people learnt the meaning of the word 'espresso'. Both my parents were among them. There was a photographer on the pavement outside, so I have photos of both Mum and Dad with their parents, snapped on different occasions, with the Repins sign hanging over their heads. Murray was harvesting poetry from the very soil from which I myself had sprung.

The poem is not a story but it makes use of one. All the crowded city venues (Tattersalls, the Greek Club) are emptying of patrons because there is a spectacle in Martin Place that everyone has to see. It is a man who is crying. We never learn his name. But his effect on the city is palpable: his emotion makes him a kind of saint. People are fascinated, yet too scared to draw near:

> but the weeping man, like the earth, requires nothing,
> the man who weeps ignores us, and cries out
> of his writhen face and ordinary body
>
> not words, but grief, not messages, but sorrow,
> hard as the earth, sheer, present as the sea—
> and when he stops, he simply walks between us
> mopping his face with the dignity of one
> man who has wept, and now has finished weeping.
>
> Evading believers he hurries off down Pitt Street.

Four decades on, Murray included this poem in *Killing the Black Dog* (2009), a book which also contains an extraordinary essay about his lifelong struggles with poor mental health and depression. He discusses his battle to come to terms with his relationship with his parents and to be a decent father, especially to an autistic son. His mother died in child-birth of a haemorrhage, leaving him an only child, because, it appears, his father was too coy to mention her crisis on an open phone line where neighbours might hear such personal information. 'An Absolutely Ordinary Rainbow' expresses a spirituality of depression. There are few writers with the poise to manage this.

The unaffected honesty of the essay 'Killing the Black Dog' puts a lump in my throat. Murray writes about being bullied at school, being callously medicated and the times when he was difficult to live with. 'The worst way to have chronic depression is to have it unconsciously, to be in a burning rage and not know you are angry.' Murray borrows the expression 'black dog' from Churchill but knows it has a long ancestry. He comes to realise that his essay should be called 'Learning the Black Dog': the bugger can't be killed but Murray is among those who have learnt to be themselves without being hounded out of their self-possession.

~

I spoke a few times with Les Murray when I was working on a book about the Hume Highway. In September 1961, he wrote one of the poems that made his name in the Halfway Café, a modest eatery in Tarcutta (population four hundred, these days). Murray was hitchhiking from Sydney to Melbourne, sleeping under trees along the way. He was a month short of his twenty-third birthday and, already becoming familiar with the demands of living with mental illness, was feeling lost and restless. He had got a lift which left him at Tarcutta and he had time to wait for another.

In the interval, he composed 'The Burning Truck'. The poem works with a disarmingly simple image. A truck catches fire, the driver jumps out, but the vehicle manages to keep going:

> And all of us who knew our place and prayers
> clutched our verandah-rails and window-sills,
> begging that truck between our teeth to halt...

'I was exalted and crazy at the time,' Les told me, 'in the manic phase, I guess, of a depressive breakdown. I'd dropped out of university, sold all my possessions, cut adrift, and had been living in Sydney as a street kid. I'd published a few poems... I was just beginning to convert a dream of being a poet into an attempt to realise the dream. My head was full of violence and war imagery—I was a little boy during World War II.'

Murray finally reached Melbourne with 'The Burning Truck' among the limited number of possessions he had: 'I polished it up...the next day and...sold it to Vin Buckley, then poetry editor of the *Bulletin*, for five pounds. That modest amount kept me fed for a week.'

After that, Murray tried his luck selling door to door.

~

When Murray's *Collected Poems* was published, in 2006, 'The Burning Truck' was the first work included. Around this time, I invited Murray to come on a radio program I was working on in Canberra. I asked him to read 'An Absolutely Ordinary Rainbow'. I heard afterwards that people stopped their cars to listen to him, just as happens in the poem. I understood now the breathless intensity of his reading. It was like finally coming to appreciate the voice of Dylan. His reading was not about self-promotion. It was an invitation to listen carefully. I did so. Looking at him in a soulless studio, I was moved by the powerful sense of humanity the poem brought with it.

Afterwards, we went out to lunch. We could have chosen from a dozen trendy cafés in the area but Les made a beeline for a fish-and-chip shop where he ordered a roast-beef roll. I don't mind this kind of cardiac catering myself, so I ordered something not dissimilar. When his food arrived, he took the lid off the salt cellar and poured salt directly onto the beef and gravy, part of which spilt onto his clothes. They looked like they had come from an op-shop and his lunch was doing nothing to enhance their appearance. He had an ageing base-ball hat on his head. I realised, if I hadn't already, that here was a man who had created some of the most elegant poetry I knew. Indeed, everything elegant about him was in his writing. His work was as fine as gossamer. It's just that his lunch wasn't.

I asked Les to sign my copy of his collected poems and he spilled gravy on the book as he did so. Then he pointed out the image on the cover: a little girl, sitting on a stool and trying to hug an enormous elephant. 'I love that picture,' he said. 'It's the best cover I've ever had.'

CHAPTER 13

The Bedside of My Mother

Simone de Beauvoir, *A Very Easy Death* (1964)

I love a good café as much as anyone else. I have sat in cafés
and marked work by students, even composed the occasional
text message—hardly a literary event. This is not much to hold
against the café output of one of the best-known couples of the
twentieth century: Simone de Beauvoir (1908–86) and her part-
time partner, Jean-Paul Sartre (1905–80). In the years during
and after World War II—they had endured the privations of
occupied Paris—they frequented cafés as they composed the
monumental works for which their names are often remembered. Beauvoir's *The Second Sex* (1949) is a feminist milestone
whose warmth and sense of universal human community
sometimes surprises readers who are expecting something
more astringent. Sartre's *Being and Nothingness* (1943) is vast.
It leaves you wondering that, if he can get a thousand pages

out of nothingness, it's just as well he didn't write a book called *Being and Somethingness*.

He called her 'the beaver' and she called him Sartre. He chose a nickname based on the English sound of Beauvoir; it was also a kind of diminutive, literally a pet name. She, on the other hand, used the same appellation for her beau that the public used: in the course of their relationship he became a public institution, so much so that when Sartre was taken into custody for civil disobedience during the widespread social unrest of 1968, the president of France, de Gaulle, released him with the statement: 'You don't arrest Voltaire.' Sartre could hardly have paid an advertising agency to come up with such an endorsement.

But when Beauvoir used the name Sartre it had the effect of taking him off his pedestal. He needed that more than he acknowledged. Sartre was famous for a philosophy whose cornerstone is the idea that we are all terrified of our freedom and accept the restraints of conventional living in order to blind ourselves to the extent of our true liberty. At times, he believed that we should always be in control of our emotions and should never be swamped by pain, a bit like a stoic (see Chapter 36).

There is much to admire about Sartre. He was generous, supported people in need and acquired little in the way of material possessions. But, for all his teaching about freedom, he was not a liberator. His curious sexual proclivities tied people up in knots. Sartre's idea of freedom was a kind of prison.

Sartre's philosophy comes through in two famous images. One occurs in his first novel, *Nausea* (1938), where a conductor on a tram notices that a seat for the passengers is actually very odd. 'It could just as well be a donkey tossed about in the water.' Conventional living has blinded him to its strangeness. Freedom lies in an appreciation of the absurdity of the world. The second image is found in *Being and Nothingness*, where Sartre describes a waiter who is acting out a role. His actions and manners convey the sense that he is performing his job as though he was on a stage rather than living a life he has orchestrated for himself. Yet I wonder if Sartre fully appreciates that we are born into a history and live in a network of relationships. None of us starts from scratch. To my mind, our freedom is often about the creative acceptance of limitation. Everyone starts somewhere and that somewhere has a huge impact on the journey that follows. Both Beauvoir and Sartre wrote searching books about their childhood years. We all could.

The affectionate names Sartre and Beauvoir used for each other say something about their relationship, too, one that is so hard to understand that they hardly understood it themselves. Few people really understand their most serious relationships and this is part of the surrender that makes them possible, mysterious and even fun. If you took time to pick the threads of most relationships, they would unravel.

Beauvoir and Sartre had many sexual relationships, sometimes with the same people as each other. Beauvoir liked both men and women. Sartre liked both women and himself. He enjoyed the chase and the flattery of conquest. He tended to lose interest at the bedroom door. He and Beauvoir had a deal that they told each other all the details; they denied that there could ever be too much information. Sartre, I suspect, was a bit of a voyeur. He spent the last years of his life almost blind. Beauvoir knew how difficult this was for him.

Sartre and Beauvoir worked hard. They were energised by ideas and both expressed them in fiction, following a long tradition of the philosopher as storyteller that goes back at least as far as Plato. Sartre never doubted that he was a genius. He describes in his memoir the discovery, fairly early in life, that he was not particularly good-looking or physically impressive. He was, like Socrates, short and ugly. But he could entice with language and for that reason his account of childhood is called *Words* (1963). It is one of the most self-questioning things he ever wrote, which is why it is such a magnetic reading experience. It is tentative and sometimes fearful, everything his philosophy tries to push from the centre.

Beauvoir, always able to call his bluff, says in *Adieux: A Farwell to Sartre* (1981) that Sartre was always able to 'think against himself', meaning he could entertain ideas he'd prefer not to. She uses precisely the same turn of phrase in her extraordinary account of the last six weeks in the life of her mother, Françoise, *A Very Easy Death*. This small book is a neglected masterpiece.

While Sartre spent years coping with the pain his mother had caused him by having the temerity to remarry, Beauvoir spent just as long coping with the pain she had caused her mother. The title of her account of childhood, *Memoirs of a Dutiful Daughter* (1958), is laced with irony. She did not become the Catholic member of the middle class her mother wanted to see. At one time she was destined for the convent, a calling that would hardly have suited her. She plotted her own course. At university, she came second in her class in demanding exams in philosophy, beaten only by the extraordinary Simone Weil. It must have been a challenging class to teach. The two Simones were very different. Beauvoir journeyed into atheism and Weil journeyed away from it. Weil didn't spend much time in cafés. If she did, she would hardly have noticed. Her powers of concentration were, shall we say, above average. If she was absorbed in study or the pursuit of an idea, she might forget to eat for days on end. Beauvoir enjoyed her physical being.

The title of *A Very Easy Death* is also heavily ironic. It comes from a nurse who, after Françoise finally passes away, remarks in an offhand manner that hers had been 'a very easy death'. Beauvoir begs to differ. Sartre says in *Words* that 'dying is not easy' and this is the theme Beauvoir explores, especially the difference between dying and death. She recalls her mother saying, 'Death itself does not frighten me; it is the jump I am afraid of.' *A Very Easy Death* is in some ways a non-fiction version of Tolstoy's *Death of Ivan Ilyich* (see Chapter 26). Both books move slowly and surely towards what Tolstoy calls 'the death of death'.

There have been a number of accounts in recent years of the journey towards death and they make for emotional reading. Atul Gawande's bestselling *Being Mortal* (2014) beautifully explores the over-medicalisation of the process of dying, which can turn the final journey into a kind of technical obstacle course rather than another stage of growth and discovery. Too much medicine can make death more traumatic than it needs to be, because the person at the heart of the mystery becomes a set of graphs and statistics rather than the subject of love. He has seen attempts to prolong life actually shorten it: 'The lesson seems almost Zen: you live longer when you stop trying to love longer.'

Beauvoir is of the same mind. Her mother had a fall at home and broke her leg; once in hospital, she was discovered to have cancer in her bowel, a sarcoma. She died on 4 December 1963, six weeks after her fall. *A Very Easy Death* is lofty in what it excludes. There is no mention of the death of JFK, which took place in the middle of this low-key saga, ten days before that of Françoise. The comparison might have been interesting: one death so private and the other so public; one sudden and the other less so; one mourned by millions, the other by dozens.

Nor does the book mention that Sartre was dealing with his own mother at the same time, and completing the final edits on *Words*, a book which had been on his mind for ten years. Sartre appears in Beauvoir's book as a mere mortal, calling cabs and offering support. At one stage, listening to music with Sartre, Beauvoir experiences 'an outbreak of tears that degenerated almost into hysteria'. Sartre responds that 'my own mouth was not obeying me anymore.' God knows what he meant, but it doesn't sound very helpful.

Beauvoir is unimpressed by mighty doctors: 'Neat, trim. Shining, well-groomed, bending over this ill-kempt, rather wild-looking old woman from an immense height: great men, bigwigs. I recognised that piddling self-importance.'

By way of contrast, the book charts a relationship being restored to life as Françoise slowly dies:

I had grown very fond of this dying woman. As we talked in the half-darkness, I assuaged an old unhappiness; I was renewing the dialogue that had been broken off during my adolescence and that our differences and likenesses had never allowed us to take up again. And the early tenderness that I had thought dead forever came to life again, since it had become possible for it to slip into simple words and actions.

A Very Easy Death sweats over a profound philosophical question. Françoise, unlike Simone, is a woman of religious faith. Her daughter respects this and is happy to facilitate a visit from a priest. But why then, if she is on the way to a better world, should Françoise cling so tenaciously to life? 'She believed in heaven, but in spite of her age, her feebleness and her poor health, she clung ferociously to this world and she had an animal dread of death.'

Beauvoir invests this question with great dignity. 'For myself,' she writes, 'I understood to the innermost fibre of my being that the absolute could be enclosed within the last moments of a dying person.' When Sartre died, in 1980, Beauvoir sat by his grave crying openly, oblivious to the vast crowds that had gathered. Her absolute was enclosed in that moment.

~

I have been in Kenya and seen women going out in the first light of dawn to pick coffee with enormous baskets strapped to their backs. I was with a group of young people in the Ngong Hills on the outskirts of Nairobi in the middle of 2014, precisely one hundred years after a complex and highly strung woman called Karen Blixen came to the area. Twenty minutes up the road is a suburb called Karen, named after Blixen, who wrote as Isak Dinesen. She is worth a chapter of her own. Her most famous book, *Out of Africa* (1937), begins with the words: 'I had a farm in Africa.' It is easy to forget that the farm in question produced coffee. 'A coffee plantation is a thing that gets hold of you and doesn't let you go,' she writes. Eventually, it went up in smoke which must, at least, have smelt wonderful.

Blixen writes of the ethereal air in the place: 'up in this high air you breathed easily, drawing in a vital assurance and lightness of heart. In the highlands you woke up in the morning and thought: Here I am, where I ought to be.' A century later, it was impossible to say, as Blixen had, that 'The air was alive over the land, like a flame burning.' The air was now darkened by diesel fumes and so full of sounds that you could almost smell them. But still women went off at dawn to pick coffee. I knew this was where I ought to be, as Blixen had, because suddenly I was seeing my life with fresh eyes.

I asked myself why the land used for coffee plantations can't be used to grow fresh fruit and vegetables for local consumption, rather than coffee for export. Kenya is the one place in the world I have seen people close to starvation. I have met people dying from AIDS whose medication was failing because it needed to be taken with food, the very thing the patient could not afford. This was not what anyone would call an easy death. Even if food were available, none of the coffee those women went out to harvest was available to them in shops and supermarkets, all of which seemed to stock Nescafé and little else. Those women were paid about four dollars a day.

On return to Melbourne, I visited one of the city's thousands of cafés. The place proudly advertised 'Single-origin Kenyan coffee'. I was pleased to make this connection with the land from which I had just returned and ordered the brew. It cost four dollars a cup, just what the pickers were paid for a day of backbreaking toil. This is what café culture has become, at least to some extent.

In Paris, there are plaques on the cafés that Sartre and Beauvoir worked out their ideas onto paper. Walking around Paris with my own family, we went past one of them, the Café Procope, which started in the seventeenth century. I presume they no longer have the original kitchen but, it being Paris, that's not a sure bet. The place has become so famous that it has become a kind of museum to itself. We didn't go in. Nor did we detour to go past the famous Les Deux Magots, even though we were in the next street. I have no idea about these particular places. I just know that too many cafés in the world take advantage of women who struggle through polluted streets at daybreak to pick coffee for a pittance.

Beauvoir says that her mother's death taught her compassion. That's what made it so hard. She comes to understand her mother's wounds. With that, the wounds of the whole world are made more visible to her. After she passes away, she describes her mother's death as 'an upper-class death'. Her emotion does not stop her thinking. She knows the poor die differently.

CHAPTER 14

The Freshness of Good

Hannah Arendt, *Eichmann in Jerusalem* (1963)

The only real argument I ever had with my friend Chris Straford was about the philosopher Hannah Arendt. We squabbled about countless trivialities, such as punctuation, sometimes for the sheer pleasure of banter, but Hannah Arendt was a real bone of contention. This isn't just because she was a smoker: photos of Hannah Arendt (1906–75) show a thin and drawn face with baggy eyes and a cigarette perched between her forefinger and middle finger as if it were an elusive idea she is trying to hold on to before it vanishes like, well, smoke. Chris, on the other hand, was as fit as a fiddle. When he was discovered out of the blue in 2016 to be riddled with cancer, he was preparing to go to Helsinki to represent his country at tennis, a sport at which he held court, so to speak. He rode his rickety old pushbike everywhere. Sometimes I would be in the car with my kids on the way to school and we would see Chris, heading in the same direction, weaving through the traffic like death couldn't touch him. My kids loved waving. I dreaded that, the way he rode, he'd be hit by a vehicle. He is the only person I've known who rode his pushbike to palliative care.

Chris and I shared an office for eight years and sometimes you could hear our laughter out in the schoolyard. Before that we had been in the Jesuit order for seven years together. We shared the same wonderful work, trying to enlarge the vision of young people who might otherwise be said to have the world at their feet. For Chris and me, a big part of this was a commitment to justice, not charity. Charity is a choice; justice is a demand. On Sunday nights, Chris would gather bread from a bakery franchise that had to be persuaded to depart from protocol and give away the bread they couldn't sell. Chris pestered them until they relented. Then, every week, he got some of our students together and took the bread around various homeless centres in the city. The bread run was the stuff of legend. Chris insisted the students talk to people, not just drop the loaves and move on. It was the talking, not the bread, that changed lives. Sometimes he brought his own children with him.

When Chris rang me to tell me how sick he was, I happened to be taking advantage of the lavish afternoon tea that was served after the funeral of a dear gentleman who had died at a ripe old age. Something in my world crumbled during that phone call.

'There will be grace in this,' said Chris. He was right, and the next six months were a hard and beautiful journey.

I took over Chris's classes, including a senior ethics group that had been studying the arguments about euthanasia. These were seventeen-year-old students and, of course, rather pragmatic in their views. Every one of them thought euthanasia was a good idea. Chris visited the class, struggling to breathe to get there, and told them about what his life was like and where it was headed. The kids did not know how to respond. Chris had muddied their waters, turned their shallow certainties into profound confusion. This is the sign of a great teacher. A black-and-white world will always be small. Chris lived in colour and wanted his students to do the same. Chris suffered fools. In fact, he loved them, which is just as well because there is no greater fool than a person who can't suffer fools. But he knew they were fools. We went to the same church and Chris always told his children, sitting in the front row, to make sure they had a decent book to read during the sermon. For him, the vital thing was the community. The self-important and insipid mush that came from the pulpit was neither here nor there.

~

Nobody could accuse Hannah Arendt of creating insipid mush. In 1954, she published 'The Crisis in Education', an essay that remains one of the most cogent reflections on the process of learning and formation I have come across. Arendt speaks powerfully to the increasingly driven and businesslike nature of schooling. She identifies the problems that arise when education focusses exclusively on training individuals so they can succeed on their own terms. She distinguishes between education and teaching, and speaks up in favour of the latter.

Teaching creates a relationship and a relationship creates a moral context: this is true learning. It is about formation of character, not calibrated results: 'one cannot educate without at the same time teaching; an education without learning is empty and therefore degenerates with great ease into moral emotional rhetoric.'

Arendt knew enough about emotional rhetoric. She wanted to re-establish trust in authority and tradition, not pander to educational fads. Arendt was a German and a Jew who, in 1940, was interned in a Nazi concentration camp in the southwest of France. She managed to escape as a refugee to the United States, where she arrived in 1941 and eventually became the first female professor of politics at Princeton. Soon after arriving, she published an article, 'We Refugees' (1943), which is more significant now than ever. She describes what happens to humans, who are inherently social, when they lose their society. It reminds us that the welfare of refugees is the welfare of us all.

'The Crisis in Education' concludes with one of the great definitions of education. Every school should have these words put up on the wall somewhere:

> Education is the point at which we decide whether we
> love the world enough to assume responsibility for it,
> and by the same token save it from that ruin which
> except for renewal, except for the coming of the new
> and the young, would be inevitable.

Chris Straford had no difficulty with this. On the contrary, he relished this kind of thinking, which came to flower in

Arendt's classic work *The Human Condition* (1958). That book presents the defence for the human family in the face of the case against, for which the previous fifty years of bloody history had provided ample evidence. It insists that humans aren't programmed.

Chris was by no means alone in his problems with Hannah Arendt. She was not keen on the idea of a Jewish homeland. She asked where the Jewish leadership had been in the face of the Nazis. She had an affair with Martin Heidegger, the philosopher who supported National Socialism. Chris was a strong and exceedingly well-informed enthusiast for Judaism. He did not like what he saw as Arendt's flirtations with something hostile to it. Most of all, he struggled with *Eichmann in Jerusalem*, a book I admire. In *The Human Condition*, Arendt says that it is in our nature for us to do surprising things. *Eichmann in Jerusalem* is surprising. It gave the world a catchphrase that resonates through every contemporary terrorist attack and gun massacre, especially when those atrocities start to follow a familiar pattern: 'the banality of evil'.

Adolf Eichmann had been a lieutenant-colonel in the SS and was one of the major organisers of the extermination of Jews as part of the Final Solution. He probably did not kill any Jews himself. He simply (if that's the right word) arranged trains and other practicalities to make sure it all happened efficiently. He drove a desk but it was a pretty nasty desk. After the war, he fled under the name of Ricardo Klement to Argentina. If he hadn't boasted of his sick exploits to a girlfriend, he may have eluded capture. But he was nabbed by Mossad in a nondescript industrial suburb of Buenos Aires in May 1960. Dr Mengele narrowly escaped his hunters in Buenos Aires around the same time.

Eichmann was put on trial in Jerusalem and Hannah Arendt sat through the whole thing, writing a series of controversial articles for the *New Yorker* that eventually became *Eichmann in Jerusalem*. She observes, 'To a Jew this role of the Jewish leaders in the destruction of their own people is undoubtedly the darkest chapter of the whole dark story.' This enabled Eichmann's behaviour. 'The most potent factor in the soothing of his own conscience was the simple fact that he could see no one, no one at all, who was actually against the Final Solution.' Chris Straford loathed this blaming of victims and he was right to do so.

But Arendt asks hard questions that are worth considering. In teaching philosophy to teenagers, I ask them to understand the story of Alan Turing, the inventor of the computer and pioneer of artificial intelligence. Turing composed a famous test that poses the question of whether or not a machine could imitate human thinking to such an extent that it would be impossible to tell one from the other. His question has a partner in Arendt's question about Eichmann. Turing asks if a machine could effectively become human. 'At one point does destroying a machine become the same as murder?' Arendt asks if a human could become a machine and hence forfeit moral responsibility. Only a person can commit moral acts. If a person is dehumanised, are they no longer a moral being?

Taken together, Turing's question and Arendt's form the philosophical core of the modern age. They are asking about human identity. What makes a human different?

The key to this, for Arendt, is language. She notes that Eichmann could only speak in clichés. This suggested to her that he was mouthing words like a tape recorder rather than thinking in any way for himself.

> Officialese became his language because he was genuinely incapable of uttering a single sentence that was not a cliché...The longer one listened to him, the more obvious it became that his inability to speak was closely connected with an inability to think.

She closely observes his execution, noting that Eichmann had no belief in any kind of God or afterlife. But on the gallows, he had nowhere to turn but to clichés. He stood erect and proclaimed, 'We shall all meet again...Such is the fate of all men.' He said of Germany and his adopted Argentina, 'I shall not forget them.' Arendt comments, 'In the face of death, he had found the cliché used in funeral oratory.'

> It was as though in those last minutes he was summing up the lesson that this long course in human wickedness had taught us—the lesson of the fearsome, word-and-thought-defying banality of evil.

Chris Straford and I spoke about this during his last few weeks. In some ways it was a distraction. He had been reading Jonathan Sacks' *Not in God's Name* (2015) and was fully alive to the mystery of life, even as he was dying. We laughed about funeral clichés and the way people pad themselves with easy sentiment in difficult situations. How could two of the trickiest ideas, thought and time, come together in an empty phrase such as 'thinking of you at this time'? If anything, the cliché 'hoping for love and peace' is also made out of three big philosophical ideas. We thought this was hysterical. It hurt Chris to laugh but he couldn't stop. Perhaps it was gallows humour.

Chris ran everywhere, which was ironic because he was always running late. He never wore a watch and seldom carried a phone. All of this stemmed from the fact that Chris was able to occupy the present moment, to be fully in the company of people without thinking about what needed to be done next. Even as he neared the end, struggling to walk as far as the bathroom beside his bed, he was fully present to you.

Two days before Chris died, Jenny and I visited him with our three children and he embraced them all. I don't think they will ever forget this moment. There were no words for it, no worn-out and familiar expressions. Chris believed in the freshness of good rather than the banality of evil. The last thing I ever heard him say was: 'The spirit is in this room.' The room in Cabrini Hospital, with its packaged food and remote-controlled TV, was certainly banal. The good that was in it was certainly not. Hannah Arendt believed that our task was to renew the world we share. Even in his death, Chris was part of that renewal.

CHAPTER 15

The Whole Story
Is the Meaning

Flannery O'Connor, *A Good Man*
Is Hard to Find (1955)

There are few people as funny as those who take themselves
too seriously. On the other hand, there are few people as serious
as those with a gift for comedy.

Flannery O'Connor (1925–64) seemed to understand this
from an early age. When she was nine, she drew a cartoon
of her parents, Regina and Edward, pillars of the community of Savannah, Georgia, where Flannery, christened Mary,
was born and raised. Regina was the Southern matron from
central casting, descended from those who survived America's
Civil War on the losing side. Edward had served in World
War I and was a local politician. He was always a bit beneath
the status of his wife, a woman for whom social propriety was
serious business and hence, for her clever daughter, extremely
funny. The cartoon shows Regina, Edward and Flannery

walking along as the mother tells them both to hold their heads up. The girl replies, 'I was readin where someone died of holding their head up.' O'Connor later wrote, 'Only if we are secure in our beliefs can we see the comical side of the universe.' The universe, for Flannery O'Connor, was a corner of the American South. Her sinewy comedy made it big.

Regina kept holding her head up, so much so that, in the years she was to spend living alone with her daughter on a farm called Andalusia near Milledgeville in Georgia, she never seemed to comprehend Flannery's exacting craft as a writer, one which involved pecking small seeds of experience from the ground at her feet. But Regina survived both Edward and Flannery, who were each to die of lupus erythematosus, sometimes called Red Wolf. Edward was forty-five and Flannery just thirty-nine.

Her father's death when she was a teenager removed from Flannery's life one of the only people that understood the cadences of her biting humour; she seldom spoke of her loss but once referred to Edward's death by describing grace as a bullet that hits you unawares. Her comedy was born of pain and a sense of exclusion, even if her exile was sometimes self-chosen. It is evident even in the offbeat cartoons she did at school and university before she turned her hand to writing. Thanks to her lupus, Flannery spent years able to walk only with the aid of crutches. Her wit, on the other hand, was always acrobatic. She wrote in her early twenties that 'only God is an atheist', because you can't really be an atheist unless you know everything. It is an observation perfectly balanced to displease believers and non-believers alike.

Flannery O'Connor was a woman of few words and with few friends. In one of her rare TV interviews, filmed in May 1951, she seemed stuck to the point of rudeness. One of her biographers, Brad Gooch, describes her as 'an interviewer's nightmare'. Asked about the origins of her first novel, the withering *Wise Blood* (1952), she said, 'Well, I thought I had better get to working on a novel, so I got to work and wrote one.' Such ineptitude in managing the media makes a welcome change from the brash self-promotion of so many writers these days who have no hesitation in crowing about less-significant work. Nevertheless, what O'Connor said was hardly true. There was nothing random, offhand or even recreational about her writing. Every word of it was hard-won. It was always a considered engagement with the surface of reality, as well as its underlying foundations. In an essay called 'The Nature and Aim of Fiction' (published posthumously under a portentous title she did not choose herself), she dwells on this:

> People are always complaining that the modern novelist has no hope and that the picture he paints of the world is unbearable. The only answer to this is that people without hope do not write novels. Writing a novel is a terrible experience, during which the hair often falls out and the teeth decay. I'm always highly irritated by people who imply that writing fiction is an escape from reality. It is a plunge into reality and it is very shocking to the system…People without hope not only don't write novels, but what is more to the point, they don't read them. They don't take long looks at anything because they lack the courage.

During the TV interview of 1951, O'Connor was asked about life at Andalusia, where the phone would not be connected until 1956. 'I don't see much of it. I'm a writer and I farm from the rocking chair.' There is more truth in this. Her writing was a kind of observant farming, harvesting the strangeness of people, many of whom found their way up the driveway of the farm, avoiding O'Connor's colourful collection of birds, especially the peacocks, as they did so. A number of her stories begin with the arrival of a stranger in the lives of isolated people. This life seemed to match O'Connor's call to ascetical creativity. She worshipped in a nearby Cistercian community. She read the works of Thomas Aquinas every night before she went to sleep. Her room was monastic in its simplicity. She followed a writerly regime as precise as the hours of a monastery. Yes, there were brushes with love but they never flourished. The only man she kissed, Erik Langkjaer, described the experience rather unkindly by saying, 'I had the feeling of kissing a skeleton.' Flannery got her revenge on him in fiction.

~

A Good Man Is Hard to Find is a mesmerising book of short stories. There is nothing quite like it, even O'Connor's post-humous collection *Everything that Rises Must Converge* (1965), a book that takes its title from an expression coined by the theologian and palaeontologist Pierre Teilhard de Chardin. Teilhard was talking about the evolutionary forces of creation struggling towards some coherent final point, an omega. O'Connor was theologically more than just literate. But she took the grand scale of Teilhard's thought and applied it to a mundane scene where a mother and son are on a bus and the mother finds she is wearing the same dress as a coloured woman. The story's sense of evolution is played in miniature. It brings a subtle eye to race relations in the South.

O'Connor never joined any bandwagon. She preferred in her letters to note, for example, that when summer got too hot for the Ku Klux Klan to burn crosses they started using portable electric red lights. She meets terror with comedy, refusing to be poisoned. We need more people like that. In another essay, 'The Fiction Writer and His Country' (1957), she laments the way in which opinions are blown about in the wind: 'We are asked to form our consciences in the light of statistics, which is to establish the relative as absolute.'

~

The story that gives her first collection its name, 'A Good Man Is Hard to Find', includes the word 'good' in its title, as does 'A Stroke of Good Fortune'. It is a word that O'Connor thought about a lot. A large part of her philosophical pilgrimage was towards understanding that little word, as well as the word on the other side of the coin, evil. Every story is masterly, including 'A Late Encounter with the Enemy', in which General Sash, a 104-year-old veteran of the Civil War, is left to die in the queue to use a Coke vending machine at a college graduation where he is supposed to be the guest of honour, only to find that he is not as highly prized as soft drink.

'The Artificial Nigger' has a title that might make contemporary readers turn away. But Toni Morrison (see Chapter 11) praises the way the N-word is used here 'constantly, even when and especially when it is unnecessary'. The story tells of a child growing up in rural poverty with his uncle, Mr Head, on his first visit to an urban area. The point of the visit, at least for the uncle, is to ensure the boy never wants to go to the metropolis ever again. He creates, says Morrison in her essay 'Being or Becoming the Stranger' in *The Origin of Others* (2017), 'the illusion of power through the process of inventing an Other'.

> Flannery O'Connor exhibits with honesty and profound perception her understanding of the stranger, the outcast, the Other. Underneath the comedy, often noted by her reviewers, lies a quick and accurate reading of the construction of the stranger and its benefits... This process of identifying the stranger has an expected response—exaggerated fear of the stranger.

The story to read again and again, however, is 'Good Country People' (a third 'good'). The thirty-two-year-old at its hub, Joy, has changed her name to Hulga, mainly because the new name is ugly and will annoy her mother, Mrs Hopewell. Hulga lost her leg in a shooting accident when she was ten. She now wears a prosthesis and has completed a PhD in philosophy, two poor accessories in the dating game. Philosophy has given her a way of describing the world in a manner to her liking: a meaningless void. Enter the stranger, a young Bible salesman. He connives to get Hulga alone in the barn, where it turns out that his mission is to steal her fake leg. 'I've gotten a lot of interesting things,' he said. 'One time I got a woman's glass eye this way.'

Hulga encounters true nihilism in the visitor. She finds that the void is not a toy. The comedy is beyond laughter and the meaning is beyond a few words. In 'The Nature and Aim of Fiction', O'Connor says:

> Some people have the notion that you read the story and then climb out of it into the meaning, but for the fiction writer the whole story is the meaning, because it is an experience not an abstraction.

This is surely true of the many layers of 'Good Country People', where none of the characters are good, except in the sense that they are good for nothing—which is, indeed, a kind of goodness. If you are good for nothing then you are good for something but the something is a nothing. This is the kind of conundrum that Flannery O'Connor loved. There are some loves that don't travel the highway of romance, preferring dusty back roads of their own.

For O'Connor, writing was about the act of seeing. She loathed the idea of writers importing a political or social agenda into fiction. She saw this as fake. People can create banner headlines so big that they hide under them. For O'Connor, fiction was all about the minutiae of life and the minutiae always show that humans are in need of more than mere humanity can provide.

> The novelist writes about what he sees on the surface, but his angle of vision is such that he begins to see before he gets to the surface and he continues to see after he has gone past it. He begins to see in the depths of himself, and it seems to me that his position there must certainly be the bedrock of all human experience—the experience of limitation or, if you will, of poverty.

In 1958, O'Connor went to Lourdes to appease other people's ideas of what miracles were all about. She was appalled by the dirty water in which invalids such as herself were expected to bathe. 'Nobody I am sure prays in that water,' she said. Yet the experience brought to light the nature, to use the word deliberately, of her faith. 'I saw nothing but peasants and was very conscious of the distinct odor of the crowd. The supernatural is a fact but it displaces nothing natural.' This is the core of Flannery O'Connor's approach to storytelling: 'The fiction writer presents mystery through manners, grace through nature, but when he finishes there always has to be left over that sense of Mystery which cannot be accounted for by any human formula.'

CHAPTER 16

Silent Voice

Thomas Merton, *The Sign of Jonas* (1953)

I met Thomas Merton in my early twenties at what was, I now see, a lonely time in my life. It was also a verbose time. I was always talking. My form of loneliness has always wanted to make a lot of noise, perhaps to put other people off the scent. A wise old man, three times my age, put a copy of Merton's fourth book, *The Sign of Jonas*, into my hands. I was captivated. It was more than that. It is a book I have turned to constantly for the last thirty years. Sometimes I look at the beautiful photo in the end papers of a man standing alone in the woods, overshadowed by the majesty of trees in winter. I start reading and never fail to fall under its spell. It is a book that has helped me understand the exciting journey from loneliness to solitude.

Thomas Merton, a Cistercian monk, made that journey. He died in a bizarre accident in Thailand in 1968, aged fifty-four, electrocuted by a faulty fan in his bathroom. There was no autopsy, so rumours spread about both murder and suicide, although these possibilities are implausible. It was unusual enough that he was in Thailand in the first place, addressing a conference on Marxism and monasticism, two isms that seldom belong together. A Cistercian monk does not normally stray from his or her monastery and, besides, Merton had for some years pursued life as a hermit in the forest of Gethsemani Abbey, in distant Kentucky. But Merton's vision was never limited by the walls of the monastery, nor even by the limits of the visible world. He became one of the significant activists of the 1960s, an interesting way to describe someone whose life was a commitment to stillness. He wrote against war, imperialism, poverty, commercial greed and other forms of madness that are too much taken for granted. He carried on an extraordinary correspondence with everyone from Boris Pasternak to Coretta Scott King. In December 1961, Merton wrote to his friend Ethel Kennedy, the wife and later widow of Robert F. Kennedy. Merton was concerned about the martial stance of her brother-in-law JFK. His words are prescient for the politics of our times:

> Why is war such a problem to us?...I wonder to what extent our ideals are now a front for organized selfishness and systematic irresponsibility...We cannot go on living every man for himself...Certainly our most basic need is for truth and not for 'images' and slogans that 'engineer consent'. We are living in a dream world. We do not know our friends or our adversaries. We are myths to ourselves and they are myths to us. And we

are secretly persuaded that we can shoot it out like the sheriffs on TV. This is not reality.

Merton's life fell into two neat halves. Until the age of twenty-seven, he was ambitious and chaotic. Having been born in France, orphaned, and educated in England, he taught literature at Columbia University in New York, where he was acclaimed as a writer of great promise. He was no stranger to loneliness. His parents were both artists, drawn into the energy of New York. His mother died when he was six; his father, a New Zealander, when he was fourteen. Merton's last memories of his father, who had a brain tumour, were of the man continuing to draw even after other abilities had left him. Merton was rootless. He was often irresponsible: he was the father of a child for whom he offered little care and who died in an air raid during World War II. Ironically, his only sibling, John Paul, was killed taking part in an air raid in 1943. The plane John Paul was flying over Germany was shot down and the younger Merton survived for some hours with a broken back in a rubber dingy floating on the English Channel, desperate for water. His older brother became an ardent pacifist. His experience at many levels led him to appreciate the difference between destruction and creativity. God became for him another name for creativity.

In December 1941, Merton entered Gethsemani, not far from Louisville, where the future Muhammad Ali was born a month later. Ali's widow, Lonnie, has pointed out resonances between the lives of these two fighters. On the surface, they were yin and yang. Underneath, they were both passionate believers whose faith concluded that all was not right with the world. In modern Louisville, Muhammad Ali Boulevard runs into Thomas Merton Square. This was the place where, visiting a doctor some years after entering Gethsemani, Merton had a vision of the whole world as a kind of monastery. A world without walls. A world that could learn to be quiet and gentle and at peace. A community of listeners.

The Sign of Jonas is based on a journal Merton kept of life at Gethsemani in the years between 1946 and 1952. I love the ways in which Merton struggles to find his own authenticity. One cold January day, he writes:

> For the first time in my life, I am finding you, O solitude. I can count on the fingers of one hand the few short moments of purity, of neutrality, in which I have found you. Now I know I am coming to the day in which I will be free of words: their master rather than their servant, able to live without them if need be. For I still need to go out into this no-man's land of language that does not quite join me to other (people) and which throws a veil over my own solitude...The speech of God is silence.

When Merton entered the monastery, he was not running away. In fact, his journey was the opposite. Cistercian spirituality, sometimes also known as Trappist spirituality, is beautiful and austere. It is a raw salad without dressing: the community lives in radical silence. At times, communities have even developed their own sign language to obviate the need for speech. On arrival at Gethsemani, Merton was amused that a sign resembling 'past your eyes' was used for milk, from 'pasteur-ised'. The community follows *The Rule of Saint Benedict*, part of which is read aloud to the monks or nuns every day as they eat in the refectory. Benedict's sixth-century rule creates a hearty balance of work and its opposite. It is one of the great documents in the history of homemaking, whose only hard and fast instruction is 'listen', the word with which the rule begins: 'Listen carefully with the ear of the heart to the advice of a father who loves you.' Benedict knew that not even the most pure spirits ever stop being human. Merton understood this. Even in the monastery, people around him could grate on his nerves. Despite a life of radical silence, monks have a close physical relationship. In the middle of January 1950, he writes:

> It is in deep solitude that I find the gentleness with which I can truly love my brothers. The more solitary I am, the more affection I have for them. It is pure affec-tion, and filled with reverence for the solitude of others. Solitude and silence teach me to love my brothers for what they are, not for what they say.

~

The Sign of Jonas was written towards the end of Merton's romance with community; he would shortly afterwards begin life in a forest hermitage on the property of the monastery. The book ends with a justly famous epilogue called 'Fire-watch, July 4, 1952'. On a hot summer's night, Merton had the duty of walking around the weatherboard monastery from top to bottom, looking for the first sign of any fire that might destroy the place. As he walks around, every corner of Gethsemani is the occasion of a memory and a prayer. Every sleeping monk is the occasion of gratitude, wonder and, yes, even befuddlement. Merton writes: 'The night, O my Lord, is a time of freedom.' I think he means it is a time to take perspective, to see things that can't be seen with the eyes. 'You, who sleep in my breast,' he continues, 'are not met with words, but in the emergence of life within life and of wisdom within wisdom.'

At the end of every school year, we take the incoming student leaders away for a few days. It is a wonderful time when young people express all the hopes that come with being seventeen and confident you can change the world. As part of the experience, some of us rise at five in the morning to visit a Cistercian monastery where a group of monks live in almost complete silence, pursuing a lifestyle that has not changed much since the eleventh century. Young people find this commitment confronting. It is far more outrageous to them than any possible expression of sexuality. Coco Chanel grew up in a Cistercian monastery; Chanel No. 5 has always struck me as an ineffable combination of silence and sex.

Br Bernie, one of the most sane people I know, is the prior of the abbey we visit at Tarrawarra, where he has lived for forty or more years. I tell the students that Bernie is one of the few friends with whom I have never argued. That is because he so seldom speaks. He describes the monastery as a 'fridge magnet', something that reminds the rest of the world that it doesn't have as much to say as it thinks it might. Bernie believes that God doesn't use many words either. His life involves listening to deep silence. The students are gobsmacked. So, each time, am I.

CHAPTER 17

Sharp Elbows and a Hacking Cough

Dorothy Day, *The Long Loneliness* (1952)

When news broke of the death of Dorothy Day, in November 1980, I was a naïve nineteen-year-old helping homeless people in the inner suburbs of Melbourne, places which were yet to see the renovator's paintbrush. Some of them still haven't. My father had died about a year before and I, a young Jesuit novice, was trying to find my way in the world before it ran me over. I had the supreme good fortune to fall in among idealistic and generous people who knew that there are lessons you can't learn from the comfort of home. For many of them, this was more than a passing stage. They never grew into those tight-fitting suits called CV and career. Their youthful idealism became middle-aged idealism and, in some cases, the idealism of old bones. Their generosity became wisdom.

One of the places I lent a hand was the House of Welcome,

which shared its name with the Houses of Hospitality that Dorothy Day started in New York in the 1930s. Its doors were open to whoever turned up for a meal or a shower, most of them from the streets and rooming houses of the area. Almost forty years later, I am still taking young students from school to help with breakfast at the House of Welcome. They are always kept busy: there is plenty of coffee to be served and a stack of pots to be scrubbed. But the place has changed. There are many more rules and regulations about the service of food and so on. I understand this. Yet I sometimes wonder if our students get to really encounter the people of the streets and rooming houses other than as clients or, worse, convenient examples from an abstract lesson about finding happiness by 'giving back'.

Dorothy Day believed wholeheartedly in the creative power of words. She started life as a left-wing journalist and also wrote fiction. The Houses of Hospitality germinated from a movement that began with a newspaper she established in 1933, the *Catholic Worker*. For her, the most important part of hospitality was conversation. She believed in sharing her table: food and talk went hand in glove. With so many strictures these days around the provision of social services, this can get lost. You can't have protocols, guidelines, professional standards or performance indicators for conversation.

I recall Dorothy Day's death made a heavy impact in that part of the world. Indeed, the death of John Lennon ten days later did not seem to strike such a tender nerve. He was a celebrity. Dorothy Day celebrated others: the poor, the voiceless, the odd, the left-out, the unlovely. People spoke of the way her inspiration had helped them to find a direction for their lives and they still discussed her visit to the district ten years earlier. Mother Teresa and Mary MacKillop were also habitués of the area. Some days you could hardly move for the number of saints wandering around. Dorothy Day said she never wanted to be treated as a saint, because 'I don't want to be dismissed that easily.' Nonetheless, I had her on a pedestal.

I was relieved then, a few years later, to encounter Chris Jenkins. He wore a straw hat in summer and a beret in winter; other than that, he was not much concerned with his wardrobe. Chris had spent some years engaged in his own heartfelt search, living for a long period in a community that was squatting in a house that had been abandoned in Quex Road, in North London. Before that, he had spent two years in Maryhouse on Fifth Street, in the Bowery district of Manhattan. You don't have to have been to New York to know there is, or was, a world of difference between Fifth Street and Fifth Avenue. Maryhouse was the place where Dorothy Day, then quite elderly, was living in retirement. Chris remembers her as 'very straightforward', a woman who spoke her mind bluntly. 'She was a lady with sharp elbows.'

Chris was assigned a bed directly beneath her room. I was impressed that he had been so close to such a personage. For him, it was a nuisance more than anything else. She coughed all night and he couldn't get any decent sleep. Her cough was persistent, a bit like everything else she did. Dorothy Day had been a career smoker. She smoked in the bath as she read fiction when she was pregnant with her daughter, Tamar Teresa. She smoked on the way to the hospital to give birth. She smoked at the dining table, hardly the most hospitable thing to do. I relished this story. It got Dorothy Day off her pedestal and brought her back to street level. You can't be properly human without getting on the nerves of at least someone. Dorothy Day got on the nerves of many. That was her job.

Her powerful autobiography, *The Long Loneliness*, gives the clear impression that a significant part of Dorothy Day's formation came through reading literature. She warmed to novelists such as Jack London and Upton Sinclair, writers who are all but forgotten now but who were prepared to ask society to look at itself. She also loved Hugo and Tolstoy (see Chapter 26), the last fuelling her lifelong commitment to non-violence and total opposition to war. Dickens crops up over and again in her writing; Dostoyevsky was a passion.

The Long Loneliness speaks a lot about Day's work and the search for a spirituality to sustain that work, a radical journey that began with her first imprisonment as a suffragette at the age of twenty, in 1917. She writes about how scared she was and how two things got her through the time in jail: books and community. These were the constants throughout her life. As she was dying, she read the letters of Flannery O'Connor (see Chapter 15).

The Long Loneliness also explores three of the most significant human relationships in Day's life. The first was with Foster Batterham, Tamar's father. Before teaming up with Batterham, Day had been through the experience of an abortion, manipulated by a man who used her badly. For her, this was such an ordeal that she wrote very little about it, dealing with it instead in the space provided by fiction.

It features in her first novel, *The Eleventh Virgin* (1924), to which a studio bought the film rights. She used the money to buy a cottage near the sea on Staten Island which she shared with Batterham, a botanist, in what she called rather coldly 'a common-law marriage'. The only hint in the autobiography of the abortion which caused her such grief is the line: 'For a long time I had thought I could not bear a child.'

Day loved Batterham and his fascination with the natural world; he got her walking in nature and this made her lungs feel better. 'If breath is life, then I was full of it.' But when Day became pregnant, he was not happy because he thought it was wrong to bring children into 'such a world as we lived in'. He was also uncomfortable with Day's rediscovery of God. So the couple split and Day brought up Tamar as a single mother. This was both the happiest and loneliest time of her life. Day was always a force to be reckoned with. As soon as she had given birth, she wrote a newspaper article from her hospital bed.

The other two relationships she dwells upon are those with Tamar, who married, had nine children, lived on a farm which was part of the hospitality movement and made the best of a frugal life. And, finally, a Frenchman called Peter Maurin, twenty years her senior and a former Christian Brother, who stepped into Day's life at the right moment. He was the philosopher and she was the person who could translate the philosophy into action. *The Long Loneliness* is made tender by the writer's affection for Maurin. His gift of the gab makes for some of the funnier moments in the book, such as when he insists on delivering an ideological address at Tamar's wedding. He could be torrential. Day's description of his dementia and loss of speech before he died is beautiful.

Soon after Dorothy Day died, I found *The Long Loneliness* sitting in the office at a community for homeless alcoholics called The Way, where I was also helping out. It wasn't an office, really, just a space under the stairs where there was a jar in which we put whatever coins we had to keep the place running. I was instantly absorbed and challenged. The book allowed me to see beauty in the chaos and broken lives around me. It took the place in my affections of a work that was published just a few months before it, in the same city, *The Catcher in the Rye* (1952). Salinger's book about phoniness is slick and sassy, and for generations thousands of its young fans boasted of being able to read it in a single sitting. *The Long Loneliness* asks far more of its readers. It asks them to build community and to make a place at the heart of that community for someone other than themselves.

CHAPTER 18

Loss

Vera Brittain, *Testament of Youth* (1933)

At one time, Jenny was teaching seven-year-old students. They were nothing if not honest, although sometimes you got the feeling their honesty was imported from home. After a long day at the zoo, one of them sat down beside her on the bus. 'Miss,' he said, 'you look like you need a beer and a back rub.'

Jenny was required to tell them about one of the great battle scenes in the history of literature, the time when the people of Israel escaped from slavery in Egypt and set out for the land promised to them. In order for them to get away, the Red Sea parted for the good guys and then closed back over the bad ones who were thrown into disarray and drowned. This is a foundational story for Muslims, Christians and Jews alike. It is told every year at Passover. Christians listen to the story at Easter. Indeed, as they prepare to celebrate their most solemn night, some Christians sing a macabre refrain: 'Horse and rider he has thrown into the sea.' I cringe every time.

It is great to celebrate a freedom story and that is, of course, what the scriptures have in mind. When it comes time for Moses to receive the Ten Commandments, they are prefaced by a reminder: 'I am the Lord your God who brought you up out of the land of Egypt.' In other words, God is a liberator. The rules and regulations are really all about preserving a hard-won freedom and they are meaningless otherwise. If the rules themselves become a source of captivity, then they are useless. We forget that. There are endless examples in the history of spirituality of people whose anxiety has turned freedom into chains.

But what about poor Pharaoh and all his soldiers and horsemen? The scriptures don't waste much compassion on them. Admittedly, holy writ has a pacifist tinge. The people of Israel are defenceless; they have no weapons and do no fighting. They don't need to. God does the fighting for them. Sadly, history is full of armies that have gone to war confident that God is wearing their uniform.

Perhaps it was with some concern for the Egyptians that Jenny asked her seven-year-old students how Pharaoh might have reacted to the bad luck that befell his army. One boy raised his hand timidly. 'Miss, miss.'

'Yes?'

'I know, miss.'

'Well, tell us.'

The boy assembled his words slowly and deliberately. 'He would have had anger-management issues.'

Well done, that boy. He was only seven but he'd learnt the professional parlance of his time. He was not to know, though, that his description and Pharaoh's disaster come from entirely different experiences of the world. The minute you say Pharaoh had 'anger-management issues' you have parked him in the HR department of a large company where he has been under-performing. If historical figures are to remain real, you need to allow them to keep their distance.

~

Literature is full of bloodshed, violence and war. This is inevitable because sadly history is also full of those things. There have been countless books written about the experience of war, most of them by men. World War I had a profound impact on the way the human family sees itself and first-hand accounts of that desperate tragedy tend to leave the reader with anger-management issues.

Testament of Youth by Vera Brittain (1893–1970) is unique among these, not only because it is written by a woman but also because that woman is strong, independent and at times fierce. Brittain began the arduous process of telling this story ten years after the Great War ended. She had tried several fictional versions but none of them worked; as much as others find that fiction strips a writer naked, she found it was possible to hide there. She had to let the facts speak for themselves. The book was published five months after Hitler came to power. It found an immediate readership among people who couldn't believe that human beings were such slow learners.

More than anything, you can actually see and feel the world changing in the course of this vast book. It begins in the

Edwardian middle class close to Newcastle. Vera's parents were impeccable period pieces. She herself struggled to win a place in Somerville College at Oxford University, no mean feat. It meant convincing her parents that she was not spoiling her marriage prospects while also cramming for tough entrance examinations. Brittain was not going to be trapped by convention. At the same time, the prose at the start of *Testament of Youth* is perfect in its Edwardian manners. It is elegant, artful and considered.

Vera's younger brother, Edward, and his best friend, Roland Leighton, enlisted in the war with the best of tally-ho motives. They wanted to do their noble duty and were joined by another school chum, Victor Richardson. Vera, caught up in their spirit of patriotic service, relinquished her place at Oxford and began a gruelling career as a Voluntary Aid Detachment nurse. She found herself junior to the permanent nurses and effectively became a servant but her stiff upper lip had not yet begun to quiver. She was already engaged to Roland Leighton and was joining him in the war effort while she awaited his return and the resumption of their high-toned careers. Roland was an aspiring poet who had gone to war with the sonnets of Rupert Brooke in his kit.

The bedside of wounded and dying soldiers was the perfect place from which to observe the truths of war and, with that, to chart the way the world moved from sunshine into shadow. *Testament of Youth* is full of extraordinary vignettes. In 1918, working in a hospital in Étaples, she notes:

> One of the dying men had his wife beside him for two
> or three days; she didn't much enjoy her vigil, and had

already begun to flirt with the orderly sergeant before
he came to superintend the removal of her husband's
body. I wondered whether she knew the dead man had
been syphilitic as well as gassed.

This is hardly the classic deathbed scene of a fallen knight
attended by his lady. There are no certainties in this account. It
is all chaos and confusion. When Brittain is called upon to nurse
German casualties, she finds their humanity is no different from
that of the English. One very attractive young German asks her
politely, with 'restless, agonised biting of his lips', how soon he
would die. 'It was not very long; the screens were round his
bed by the next afternoon.' There is an equally telling moment
when the Armistice is finally signed and the world begins to
celebrate. Brittain starts to walk towards the festivities:

> The next moment there was a cry for doctors and nurses
> from passers-by, for in rounding the corner the taxi had
> knocked down a small elderly woman who in listening,
> like myself, to the wild noise of a world released from
> nightmare, had failed to observe its approach.

The unfortunate woman is killed the moment peace has been
achieved. It is a scene from the theatre of the absurd, a sign that
the world will not return to the same order and predictability
as before.

Geoffrey Thurlow was a close friend and fellow officer
of her brother, Edward. These four young men—Geoffrey,
Edward, Roland, Victor—had been Vera's world. Roland was
killed on 23 December 1915. His fiancée received the news as
she was waiting for him to come home on leave to celebrate

Christmas. When his kit was returned, it was still covered in mud. His clothing smelt so bad that his mother burnt it. Victor was injured and lost his eyesight. Vera decided, as an act of reparation, that she would marry him instead and care for him for the rest of his life. But in 1917, he also died. Days later, Geoffrey, too, was killed in action.

Finally, Vera was improbably reunited with Edward in hospital before he was able to return to the Italian front. He was shot by a sniper on 15 June 1918, just a few months before the end of hostilities. He had been decorated with a Military Cross, but such honours had well and truly begun to pale by now. After his death, Vera went and found Edward's commanding officer, convalescing in hospital, and tried to find out more, but Colonel Hudson, only twenty-six, a career officer, was tight-lipped. Edward's mother did not want to know any details. 'So whether Edward's part in the vital counter-attack on the Plateau really involved some special heroism, I shall never know.'

Years later, thanks to the persistence of Mark Bostridge, who tracked down Hudson's son and his journal, Edward's story did emerge. Hudson had told Captain Brittain that he was about to face a court-martial for having gay sex. This could have meant execution and certainly would have meant shame on his name and family. So he either deliberately put himself in harm's way or committed suicide while appearing to do so—he had been shot in the head. Mrs Brittain had guessed what had happened. One can only wonder how many gay people had been in the same predicament.

~

Testament of Youth charts the author's post-war journey towards pacifism. It includes her marriage to a gentleman who did not want to be named in the text, and charts her ambitions as a writer and her ambivalence about sex, marriage and religion. It is, above all, a profoundly feminist work, recording, for example, the way that women's suffrage slipped into law in the dying months of the war:

> With an incongruous irony seldom equalled in the history of revolutions, the spectacular pageant of the women's movement, vital and colourful with adventure, with initiative, with sacrificial emotion, crept to its quiet, unadvertised triumph in the deepest night of wartime depression.

Brittain gives voice to the experience of millions of women:

> What exhausts women in wartime is not the strenuous and unfamiliar tasks that fall upon them, nor even the hourly dread of death for husbands or lovers or brothers or sons; it is the incessant conflict between personal and national claims that wears out their energy and breaks their spirit.

Testament of Youth bears witness to the tumultuous birth of the modern world. Vera Brittain presents herself warts and all. That is why everything about this book seems so trustworthy—and rebuilding trust became Brittain's life's work. She managed her anger sufficiently to find a new beginning.

CHAPTER 19

Exquisite Moments

Virginia Woolf, *Mrs Dalloway* (1925)

I live in a house that was built in 1925, the same year that Virginia Woolf (1882–1941) published her fourth novel, *Mrs Dalloway*. The book and the house have each helped me to understand the other. Fiction can do that. It makes things up but in so doing it sheds light on reality, often in unexpected ways. Fiction is really about discovery more than invention.

We chose our house for convenience. It had the right number of bedrooms and space out the back to put a trampoline so our three rapidly growing children could reach new heights or at least let off steam. It had running water, electric light, opening doors and closing windows, and was close to schools and the train. The area happened to be a byword for respectability, as is Woolf's character of Clarissa Dalloway. We settled in a place only fifteen minutes' walk from the largest shopping centre in the southern hemisphere, a place where you can get all the unnecessities of life. Every year, our street does Christmas lights with gusto, and visitors walk up and down to admire them, pointing us out to their friends as curiosities. 'Oh, look, those people must live there.' At Halloween, we are surprised by the number of children who turn up in plastic costumes, as we don't see these kids during the year: we assume they must get driven to their music lessons and thus became invisible. They are certainly more used to treats than tricks. This is a part of the world in which Christmas and Halloween and various other days are mainly consumer events. I suppose most of the world is like this now. But we inhabit a privileged area and we are fortunate to have been able to sneak in. For months after we arrived, I felt like I was living in someone else's house, possibly one belonging to an elderly aunt.

All this changed the Christmas we invited John Doenau for lunch. Jenny and I both knew John before we met each other but we hadn't run into him for ages. By this stage John was eighty-four and living in retirement on another other side of town. As I went to pick him up, I realised why Santa chooses Christmas to deliver his presents. The traffic is so much better on a public holiday.

John took time to get into the car, as his legs were not what they used to be. 'Where do you live?' he asked.

I named the area.

'That's funny. That's where I grew up.'

'Oh, really. What street?'

'You'd never have heard of it. It's only a little street.'

It turns out that not only had I heard of the street, I lived in it. As we turned the corner, we paused outside the house in which John took his first steps, in 1929. He spoke about his father, who had seen action at Gallipoli in 1915 and was still going, having been promoted only one rank, when the Armistice was signed in 1918. He then took up a job in the public service. John explained that the whole street had been built as housing for returned soldiers; the buildings were made of weatherboard because they were designed for enlisted men as opposed to officers, who were entitled to brick. In the 1920s, this was literally the last street in the city: on the other side of the road, the dairies and orchards began. John often walked the seven kilometres from here to school; he attended the school at which I was then teaching, another coincidence.

When we pulled up outside our place, a few doors further down, John had trouble walking even from the gate to the front door. He leant on my arm so he could climb the two steps.

He stopped short. I thought he might have been unwell.

'I know this place,' he said, looking around. 'Yes, I know this place, for sure. This was where the Franklins lived.'

As a toddler, John often came to our house. His mother, Mrs Franklin and another woman across the road lived with husbands who lived with the aftermath of war and were unable to sleep. They established an informal support group and met in our house, with their children, almost every working day. They took turns to catch some sleep while one of them minded the children. They each understood what it was like to be married to a man who, in the euphemism of the day, 'couldn't settle'—an expression to describe post-traumatic stress. Eighty years later, the experience was sitting low down in John's memory. He spoke about it as if it was yesterday. 'I crawled on this floor,' he said.

That story changed my relationship with the house. I was living in a place with a history of pain and struggle. This was precisely what Virginia Woolf was dealing with in *Mrs Dalloway*: the pain that endures beneath the unruffled exterior of a respectable existence.

~

It's hard to think of a writer who can achieve as much in two hundred pages of prose as Virginia Woolf. Writing was costly for her. Her mental health was always fragile and her work was created with such exquisite obsession that there's no doubt she could have found much safer ways to spend her time. This is not to say that she lacked a sense of humour. Works such as *Orlando* (1928) and *Flush* (1933) are achingly funny. Parts of *Mrs Dalloway* are funny, too, especially when Woolf is scratching at the pretensions of those whose lives will continue, war or no war, according to comfortable social niceties. But Woolf was never afraid of the deep, no matter what it took to move beyond her depth. People have remarked upon the macabre appositeness of the fact that she drowned herself in 1941. She'd spent most of her life drowning, in a sense. Her work is witness to this and, for me, *Mrs Dalloway* is its high-water mark.

It is too easy to attach labels to Virginia Woolf. She has been described as bipolar, a term which, in itself, needs a lot of unpacking. Both her parents had been widowed before they married each other. Her father, Sir Leslie Stephen, was a distinguished intellectual, the editor of Britain's celebrated *National Dictionary of Biography*. He was a strident atheist and prone to fits of bone-shaking rage, especially when under pressure of work. His daughter Laura (Virginia's half-sister) had a series of mental-health problems and spent years in what, in those days, were called asylums. Virginia's mother, Laura, died when she was thirteen. Her half-sister Stella, who filled part of the vacancy left in Virginia's life by the death of her mother, married and died within three months when Virginia was fifteen. Virginia was sexually abused by both her half-brothers, George and Gerald. All these things happened before she reached adulthood. It is no surprise that her own mental health was, to use a polite expression, delicate.

Virginia married Leonard Woolf in 1912 and the pair started the Hogarth Press, one of the defining moments in the cultural history of the twentieth century. Woolf won some of the money for this venture in a sweepstakes on the Melbourne Cup. Tolstoy and Dostoyevsky might have applauded the rare contribution of something positive from gambling to the life of writers. Almost as soon as Virginia and Leonard married, she fell into a series of breakdowns that lasted well into the Great War and the Hogarth Press was initiated to some extent as occupational therapy.

Leonard was a patient and stabilising influence throughout her life. He seemed to understand the intellectual and sexual intimacy she shared with Vita Sackville-West and several others. *Orlando*, which is dedicated to Sackville-West, is a delicious celebration of fluid sexuality. The most engaging erotic experience in the life of the rather proper Clarissa Dalloway, married to the even more proper Richard Dalloway, MP, occurred many years ago when, as a young woman, she was infatuated with the vibrant and flirtatious Sally Seton, a girl who left a bathroom naked and dared to speak of the pregnancies of unmarried women. Sally kissed her on the lips and gave her a flower. Years later, Mrs Dalloway is still arranging flowers, still living in the moment she shared with Sally.

Virginia Woolf was less immediately affected by the war than were millions of others. But *Mrs Dalloway* deals with its aftermath brilliantly, partly because Woolf's own experience of mental suffering opened a door to understanding the soldiers who survived physically but returned as different people emotionally to the ones who went away. There was nothing remotely great about the Great War. Its shadow still falls on us, even after one hundred years. It shook the ground under some of the most significant foundations of western culture and identity. What vocabulary could possibly describe such horrors? How could language deal with atrocities that lay beyond the realm of thought? Of the thousands of memorials erected in the years immediately after the war, few offer any explanation of what happened. Many merely say 'Lest We Forget', and include the dates of the conflict and the names of the dead. One soldier, Ludwig Wittgenstein, grappled with the philosophy of language. His *Tractatus Logico-Philosophicus* was published in 1922. In that same year, the Woolfs' Hogarth Press published a work by a member of what was becoming known as the Bloomsbury Group, their wide circle of unusual and creative friends. It was *The Waste Land* by T. S. Eliot, a work which encounters the new world as 'a heap of broken images'.

~

Mrs Dalloway is the brilliant product of a broken world. It follows a day in June 1923 when Clarissa Dalloway is to give a brilliant evening party for people who matter, including the British prime minister. It is similar but different to the other great life-in-a-day book of that period, James Joyce's *Ulysses*, published in 1922, the year in which literature seemed to realise that a species which is prepared to destroy itself can't be represented by the neat structure of a Victorian or Edwardian novel with a beginning, middle and end, and a narrator who can reliably tell the whole story. *Ulysses* is an extraordinary casserole of high culture and scatological inanity, mystical insight and urban drudgery. It suggests that a single day in the life of an ordinary man, Leopold Bloom, will evade the net with which a writer sets out to capture it. Even Bloom's penchant for eating offal stretches conventional prose. Woolf did not much like the verbal pyrotechnics of *Ulysses*. She described Joyce as 'a queasy undergraduate squeezing his pimples'.

Mrs Dalloway uses a new way of storytelling, one in which the perspective of the book slides around. It follows two parallel narratives. The first concerns Mrs Dalloway's preparations for her party, which are intruded upon by the return from India after five years of the man she ought to have married, Peter Walsh. (Leonard Woolf surrendered a lucrative civil-service post in what was then Ceylon to pursue his relationship with Virginia.) She is also concerned about her daughter, Elizabeth, who has come under the antisocial influence of an evangelical Christian called Miss Kilman. Woolf works hard at describing the nature of belief and Miss Kilman is an unsympathetic character but no stereotype. There is a superb account of her trying to pray in Westminster Abbey near the tomb of the Unknown Warrior, wondering what prayer was doing to the people in the church around her. 'Yet to others God was accessible and the path to him was smooth.'

Woolf was loyal to the fierce atheism of her irascible father. But she also strove to describe matters of spirit and wrestled with Leslie Stephen's sharply defined ideas of rational being. He had a linear view of life, represented by his *National Dictionary of Biography*. For his daughter, on the other hand, a whole world could be contained within a single experience, such Clarissa's kiss with Sally Seton. Arriving home from shopping, she thinks: 'moments like this are buds on the tree of life, flowers of darkness they are.'

A friend and colleague of mine, Daryl Barclay, has counted more than seventy occasions in *Mrs Dalloway* where Woolf uses the word 'moment'. He even had a fridge magnet made to give to his literature students in their final year of school when they were studying the book. He had printed on it the words from early in the book 'one must pay back from this secret deposit of exquisite moments.' Daryl had found a delightful ploy to get the students to notice one such moment for themselves. He has the gift of being able to help young readers take possession of works that come from miles outside their experience, and own them to such an extent that they are taken into their being and become part of their experience.

Woolf's spirituality, as it is for most people, is closely connected to her sexuality. You seldom find an authentic version of one without an honest experience of the other. Both were areas in which Woolf was prepared to voyage out. It is easy to use the label 'bisexual' to describe her. But there needs to be another word as well, a more important word. I would call it 'bi-gnosticism'. This is the ability to both believe and disbelieve at the same time. I think Virginia Woolf was bi-gnostic. It is her most outrageous quality, far more than her sexuality.

The second major narrative journey of *Mrs Dalloway* concerns Septimus Warren Smith, a soldier who has returned from the war and whose post-traumatic stress, known in those days as shell shock, leads to his suicide. *Mrs Dalloway* is riddled by the disaster of the war. It describes the blind energy required to keep the seemly rituals of life alive. Near the start of the book, we are confronted by this moment: 'Lady Bexborough who opened a bazaar, they said, with the telegram in her hand, John, her favourite, killed; but it was over; thank Heaven—over.'

News of Smith's suicide reaches Mrs Dalloway's elegant party late in the day and this is one of the small number of points at which his story connects with hers, each time with a mere feather's touch. Smith is accompanied throughout the novel by his anxious wife, Rezia, who wonders what happened to the man she met and fell in love with in her native Italy: 'He wasn't Septimus any longer.' Smith sits in the park and hallucinates about dead comrades such as Evans who seems to appear to him. Dr Holmes insists over and over that there isn't anything wrong with him. An expert, Sir William Bradshaw, condescends to give him three-quarters of an hour and believes that Septimus is lacking a sense of 'proportion, divine proportion'.

These withering portraits of the medical profession may reflect some of Woolf's own experience of coping with mental illness in the face of callous ignorance. But they break open a moment in time and peer beneath the surface of one of the defining experiences of the twentieth century.

> The word 'time' split its husk; poured its riches over him and from his lips fell like shells, like shavings from a plane, without his making them, hard white imperishable words, and flew to attach themselves in an ode to Time; an immortal ode to Time.

Words no longer do what they once did. The search for meaning, purpose and love has become a journey with far less reliable maps than those available to an earlier generation.

Mr and Mrs Franklin, who once lived in the house where my family is rapidly growing up, remind me of Septimus and Rezia: their memory is a gift. The respectability of our street is only a coat of paint.

CHAPTER 20

Not of Ourselves

Mary Gilmore, *The Passionate Heart* (1918)

Mary Gilmore (1865–1962) lived for almost a century. The portrayals of her on Australia's ten-dollar note give some idea of her span of years. In the background is the picture of a formidable old lady, based on a famous portrait by William Dobell. This is Dame Mary Gilmore, an icon of Australian culture, especially in the years after World War II. In the foreground is a much younger but no less formidable woman. This is Mary Cameron, a schoolteacher originally from Wagga Wagga, on the banks of the Murrumbidgee. She was lucky as a young woman not to marry Henry Lawson, her contemporary and fellow writer. Lawson was trouble. His life was spent in penal servitude to grog. Cameron was an idealist who, in the 1890s, became part of William Lane's New Australia settlement in Paraguay. Here she got engaged to another child of the bush, the labourer William Gilmore. Gilmore also battled the bottle.

Mary Gilmore became one of Australia's more observant characters. In 1921 she returned to Goulburn, on the Southern Tablelands of New South Wales, where she had spent a good part of her childhood. She spent most of the next four years there and discovered that the road beneath her window, which linked Sydney and Melbourne, was a constant source of fascination. She watched it the way others watch fish in a tank.

From 1908 to 1931, Mary Gilmore edited the 'Women's Page' in the *Australian Worker* and through it exerted an unacknowledged influence in the first half of the twentieth century by introducing her blue-collar readership to a broader sense of life's possibilities, without, at the same time, urging them to buy anything. If it hadn't been for the success of Gilmore in the *Australian Worker*, the *Australian Women's Weekly* might never have taken off and become arguably the most formative cultural influence in post-war Australia. Gilmore also wrote some exquisite poetry, the best of it deceptively slight.

She had returned to Goulburn for a respite from the demands of living in Sydney. Her nerves were on edge; she was highly strung and prone to depression. While in Goulburn she wrote:

> I came home and looked out my window very tired
> and feeling a little strange in a world I should know
> so well. There is an ache and an emptiness…Life is
> filled with things as a shelf is filled with empty tins…

In its continual doing, even the heart itself refuses to
remember that it is hungry and starved.

Gilmore had packed both her husband, Will, and son, Billy,
off to Queensland, where they worked on the land to support
her financially while she pursued a literary career. She felt
uneasy about that. By the time she got to Goulburn, she
hadn't seen Will for eleven years or Billy for eight.

~

Mary Gilmore viewed life from the first floor, the perfect
vantage point for not just observation but also insight. She
was slightly above the common sod but not in the clouds.

From 1933 until her death, a period of about thirty years,
she lived in a small first-floor flat on Darlinghurst Road in
Sydney's Kings Cross, almost directly above the current site of
the railway station. From her balcony there, she looked out on
one of the busiest streets in town and recorded what she saw:
the Depression, World War II, and the burgeoning tourist
and sex industries all paraded beneath her unflinching gaze.

In early 1990, I visited Kings Cross and noticed that
Gilmore's flat was on the market. I rang the agent, pretended
I was a potential buyer and was shown through the property.
This may have been a little dishonest but I just wanted to
see the world from Gilmore's angle, even for a moment. Her
balcony had been enclosed and the rooms had been done
out in pastel pinks, which were the hideous contribution of
the period to interior design. There was no trace of Mary
Gilmore's signature clutter, no sign of the sofa buried under
books nor of the desk buried under paper and absolutely no

sign of the pots she used to make jam over a single gas burner. Making jam was one of her strategies when depressed.

'Is this the kind of thing you were after?' the agent asked me.

I looked at the walls. 'Not really.'

As a younger woman returning to Goulburn, Gilmore had taken a first-floor room at the Imperial Hotel, on the corner of Verner and Auburn streets, the latter the name the Hume Highway trades under when it comes to town. Gilmore's view of the highway got her thinking and, during a cold winter, she wrote an essay about it, published in 1922 in a collection called *Hound of the Road*:

> There are some people for whom a road never lived. To them it is nothing but a dull dead place of ruts upon an equally dull dead earth…Give a man a road and he has a library which neither comes to an end nor grows cheap and common. I know roads. History lies written in them for those who can read.

Gilmore's observations were often nostalgic; she was always old enough to remember when things were different, and this is a constant theme in her writing. As she got older, the gap between then and now widened. She had childhood memories of travellers on the road beneath her window. Her pioneers were haunted men who wore amulets and saw the country on either side of the road as peopled by supernatural beings. The wilderness was only a few steps from the track and in the wilderness they expected to encounter both God and Satan.

The Imperial was demolished to make way for a motel, which later had a Thai restaurant on the first floor, roughly where Mary Gilmore used to sit.

~

There is more to Mary Gilmore than nostalgia. She gave voice to the pain and neglect suffered by women who were required to accommodate the wild dreams and poor behaviour or menfolk. One of her most memorable poems, 'Eve Song', appears in *The Passionate Heart*, first published in 1918 as a dreadful war came to an end. The poem surely reflects the sense of abandonment experienced by women in time of conflict and violence. But it also captures the ambivalent feelings of someone entwined in a relationship which is liberating for only one of the people in it.

> I span and Eve span
> A thread to bind the heart of man;
> But the heart of man was a wandering thing
> That came and went with little to bring:
> Nothing he minded what we made,
> As here he loitered, and there he stayed.

The Passionate Heart was Gilmore's second book of poems and remained her favourite. She was later frustrated by her inability to replicate some of its lyrical poignancy. But it led to her being able to cross the bridge from journalism to literature. Its success, especially with critics, gave her confidence.

The real success of *The Passionate Heart* is its ability to bring darkness to light. Mary Gilmore is, to my knowledge, the first Australian writer to deal in an open and fearless way with the challenge of living with depression. She was much honoured but very often lonely: admired but alone. Many people have dealt with 'the dark Untold' by flight. This is especially a theme in the masculine myth of Australian conquest. But Mary Gilmore is a still figure. She never ran. She was at home with herself and, in so being, drew from outside herself. Her poem 'Heritage' expresses this need for connection and community:

> Not of ourselves are we free,
> Not of ourselves are we strong;
> The fruit is never the tree.
> Nor the singer the song.

CHAPTER 21

The Best of All
Impossible Worlds

G. K. Chesterton, *Charles Dickens* (1906)

G. K. Chesterton (1874–1936) wrote a number of short books about writers. He needed the money. But his work on Dickens was a labour of love. Dickens unlocked the whole world for Chesterton in a way he has done for countless others. Chesterton's *Charles Dickens* is a letter of thanks written to a rescuer.

My copy was lying on the shelves of a second-hand bookshop in Harden, a small town on the railway in the Central West of New South Wales. My father worked on a farm there during World War II but this book long precedes him. It is a colonial edition printed in 1907. On the flyleaf, Henry Swan has indicated that he took possession of the book on 26 September 1907. A few pages further on, he has included a sticker celebrating the centenary of Dickens' birth, in 1912.

Swan liked this book and I suspect I would have liked Swan. At the end, he has written the precise date on which he finished each reading. The first of those was 27 September 1907, the day after he bought it. He read it twice more the following year and once in 1909. Then he writes: 'once at least in 1910. I think more.' He read it in April 1911 and June 1915, 'and some time which I have not noted between 1911 and 1915'. So Swan read the book at least eight times before 1915 was out. I feel a kind of intimacy with Swan as a result of these dates. Intimacy always happens in detail. I know what a fellow fan of a particular book was doing on a certain day more than a century ago.

This edition includes a full catalogue of all the books Methuen is willing to send out to the colonies, including many school textbooks. After these mundane pages (which Chesterton would have cheerfully enjoyed) Swan has pencilled a list of the pages of the text that have meant most to him and finally concluded, 'The chapter (XI) on optimism is a great chapter.' I couldn't agree more. Swan has relished Chesterton's famous conclusion to that chapter: 'It is the best of all impossible worlds.' He has written in the margins at different points in it, 'Oh, I say!' and 'That is profound' and 'Here is more perception of history than in a dozen books on demonology.'

As he begins the essay, Chesterton writes about fashionable cynicism:

> The fierce poet of the Middle Ages wrote, 'Abandon hope all ye who enter here,' over the gates of the lower

world. The emancipated poets of to-day have written it over the gates of the world. But if we are to
understand the story which follows, we must erase
that apocalyptic writing, if only for an hour...Dream
for one mad moment that the grass is green...deny
that deadly knowledge that you think you know...give
up the very jewel of your pride; abandon hopelessness,
all ye who enter here.

Next to the phrase about the 'emancipated poets of to-day',
Henry Swan has written 'Yes, the dogs.' I love a reader who
talks back to books. Even better when one barks back.

~

Two of the more heartfelt literary essays of the twentieth
century are about Dickens. The other one was published in
1939 by George Orwell, the pen name of Eric Blair (1903–
50). Any reader of Orwell's *Nineteen Eighty-Four* (1949) will
soon discover the ways in which Orwell, like Chesterton,
dreads the diminishment of language. In some respects, the
novel dramatises the theories that Orwell outlined in his
masterly essay 'Politics and the English Language' (1946).
Orwell says that 'one ought to recognise that the present
political chaos is connected with the decay of language' and
that people desperate for good sense get 'a lump of verbal
refuse': 'the slovenliness of our language makes it easier to
have foolish thoughts.'

In *Nineteen Eighty-Four*, an entire language, Newspeak,
is created to control thought. If you look up a half-decent
thesaurus, you will find scores of words that could mean
'good', each with a slightly different shade of meaning or

each appropriate in a different context. The same applies to the word 'bad'. In the world of Big Brother, these will all be reduced to 'good', 'plus good' or 'double plus good'. The opposite will be 'ungood'. As one party enthusiast says, 'The destruction of words is a beautiful thing.' Language, for Orwell, is under threat and he prepares to defend it behind walls of solid common sense and plain speaking. Faced with the same challenge, Chesterton wants to leave language exposed to every absurdity that the world can hurl at it.

It's a pity that Orwell simply didn't seem to 'get' Chesterton, but nor did he understand either Tolstoy (see Chapter 26) or *King Lear*. Anything inherently comic eluded him, most of all Dickens. To Orwell, Dickens is an angel from the other side, 'a man who lives through his eyes and ears rather than through his hands and muscles'. He professes a grudging admiration for Dickens, especially for his depictions of childhood, but criticises him for a lack of concrete thinking, an inability to propose detailed social reform and a lack of rapport with the economic lives of the working classes, believing 'individual kindliness is the remedy for everything.'

Chesterton's shimmering essay about Dickens was written before Orwell's but seems to respond to most of what Orwell wrote. Chesterton said of Dickens that 'If he learnt to whitewash the universe, it was in a blacking factory that he learnt it.' Chesterton believed laughter reaches within and 'Exaggeration is the definition of art.' He suggests Dickens was 'always most accurate when he was most fantastic' and that he was 'ridiculous in order...to be true':

> The chief fountain in Dickens of what I have called
> cheerfulness, and some prefer to call optimism, is
> something deeper than a verbal philosophy. It is…an
> incomparable hunger and pleasure for the vitality and
> the variety, for the infinite eccentricity of existence.

Much as I love Orwell, I am firmly on the side of Chesterton when it comes to this. Dickens has been one of the liberators of my life. The first time I laughed aloud with a book in my hands was as a sixteen-year-old who had stumbled into *The Pickwick Papers* when he should have been playing sport before school; I still haven't fully found my way out of Dickens.

CHAPTER 22

A Local Habitation
and a Name

Joseph Furphy, *Such Is Life* (1903)

Mark Twain claimed to be the first author in history to submit a typewritten manuscript. Technology did little to enhance his prose, but Twain loved gadgets.

The manuscript of *Tom Sawyer* was, as the word implies, written longhand. Originally, Aunt Polly was introduced as she asked of young Tom, 'Where is that boy?' Twain crossed out those words and replaced them with Polly's now-famous utterance: 'What's gone with that boy?' The reader hears Polly's voice a page before learning her name. It's Polly's voice which creates her character. Twain is renowned for having something to say about everything. But his genius came from his ability to listen. He heard voices and they were real.

Twain shared that capacity with an Australian writer who rivals Twain's brand of mercurial genius: Joseph Furphy.

Furphy is really known for a single book. *Such Is Life* has frustrated and infuriated readers down the decades with its tangled plot, recondite humour and long-winded digressions on every subject from the practical to the arcane, from mechanics to philosophy. At the same time, the book has won a band of admirers who place it in a class of its own in the history of Australian writing. I am one of the latter, though I have served my time among the former. It is a book worth the struggle. At some point most readers stop scratching their heads and break into laughter. For some reason, that moment for me was when the narrator, Tom Collins, offers his views on the oxide of hydrogen. He means water. In a book about bullockies, a species of worker which no longer exists, set during the drought and depression of the early 1890s, I was able to recognise something of my own pretentiousness.

Tom Collins is a man of such absurd modesty that, in the company of bullockies, he insists on using 'sanguinary' for 'bloody' and 'sheol' for 'hell'. In one of the best-known passages of the book, he finds himself skulking naked along the banks of the Murray because his clothes are on their way to South Australia, lost in the river. Collins can't bring himself to mention by name the item of clothing, essential to his dignity, which he spends the next thirty pages trying to secure. But later in the book, he finds himself standing naked in front of Nosey Alf Morris, a stockman whom the reader has long ago realised is a woman in disguise. Collins himself is oblivious to this. Gender identity is one of the recurring themes of *Such Is Life*. Collins' horse is called Cleopatra. It is actually a stallion.

Few of the female characters in *Such Is Life* can be trusted. Collins tries to blacken his own name to avoid marriage; one memorable character, Warrigal Alf, discourses at length on a series of unfaithful wives. Some readers have wondered if such attitudes reflect Furphy's frosty marriage to Leonie Germain, a union which lasted for over forty years but which brought neither of them much peace. Leonie was sixteen, French and Catholic when they married in 1867. Furphy was twenty-four, Australian and Protestant. Throughout his life, Furphy pursued a number of platonic relationships with younger women, trying to find what was lacking in his marriage. One was with a schoolteacher, Kate Baker. Another was with Miles Franklin. He did not fully appreciate the effect these relationships had on the women concerned, especially on Baker. Needless to say, we never hear much of Leonie's side of the story. Doubtless, she could have written a counter-piece called *C'est la vie*.

Such Is Life purports to be a series of random extracts from the diary of a minor bureaucrat moving pointlessly around the Riverina region of New South Wales: 'Contrary to usage, these memoirs are published, not "in compliance with the entreaties of friends", but in direct opposition thereto.' There is little that is random about the architecture of the book. Collins is not Furphy. He is more outgoing and ebullient than his creator, a man whom people invariably came to remember as quiet. Collins' opinions do sometimes coincide with those of Furphy, but are usually delivered with a kind of throwaway self-deprecation.

Furphy's views on social justice were firmly held. They derived from his first-hand experience of the hardship endured

by working people. They also came in part from his unself-
pitying acceptance of the limitations of his own life. Furphy
developed a kind of comic stoicism which has become the
stock in trade of Australia's most searching humour. Furphy
was the forerunner of Barry Humphries and John Clarke. He
pioneered their kind of intellectual anti-intellectualism. They
always create the illusion that the joke is on them.

At the beginning of *Such Is Life*, the narrator indicates
that his purpose is to 'afford to the observant reader a fair
picture of Life as that engaging problem has presented itself
to me'. Joseph Furphy's life presented problems of its own. He
was the least successful member of a successful family and
known to them as 'poor John'. The fatalism which underlies
the humour of *Such Is Life* owes a lot to this. His parents were
among the early settlers of Port Phillip and slowly improved
their fortunes, first as part of a Scottish enclave in the Yarra
Valley and then at Kyneton. Furphy's brother, John, ran a
successful foundry in Shepparton. It was he who invented and
marketed the legendary Furphy Water Cart. During World
War I, troops used to gather around these carts to exchange
rumours and gossip. Unreliable stories have since been known
in Australia as furphies.

The two brothers were rock and water. John was a pillar
of the Protestant ascendancy, whereas Joseph thought long
and hard about the beliefs of the underclass. The long intellectual agenda of *Such Is Life* includes Christian socialism: 'the
Light of the world, the God-in-Man, the only God we can ever
know, is by His own authority represented for all time by the
poorest of the poor,' muses Collins, speaking on this occasion

for Furphy. Quoting *A Midsummer Night's Dream*, he says, 'The kingdom of God is within us; our all-embracing duty is to give it form and effect, a local habitation and a name.'

Elsewhere, *Such Is Life* deals with the ageless question of free will and determinism, whether our lives are created by our own choices or by circumstances beyond our control. Collins puts forward a theory of 'the controlling alternative', an idea that free choices actually create the circumstances which restrict us, and vice versa. Typically, this idea is played out first in the tragic circumstances which attend the death of a swagman and then in the comic circumstances which attend the loss of Collins' clothes.

Joseph Furphy tried his luck as a selector but lost his land. He then spent four years as a carrier in the Riverina, based in Hay, a disastrous time which nevertheless yielded much of the raw material for both the characters and politics in *Such Is Life*. Finally, with nowhere to turn, and a wife and three children to support, Joseph took a job as a mechanic in John's foundry in Shepparton. He stayed there for twenty years, working up to fifty-four hours over a six-day week. His comfort was to retreat to his 'sanctum', a corrugated-iron shed against the fence at the back of his cottage in Welsford Street. It was here that he read and wrote. He became a contemplative. That shed was a cave in the desert.

In April 1897, an enormous handwritten manuscript turned up in Sydney at the office of J. F. Archibald, then editor of the *Bulletin*. It was accompanied by a brief note: 'I have just finished writing a full-sized novel: title, "Such Is Life", scene, Riverina and northern Vic; temper, democratic; bias, offensively Australian.' The manuscript was twelve hundred pages of copperplate. It took another six years for the work to see the light of day. By that time, Furphy had got a typewriter and rapped the whole thing out again.

Such Is Life delights in language, in the rhythms of thought and speech. Despite the assessment of one early reviewer, Banjo Paterson, that 'its literary methods are poor and its powers of reproducing dialect phonetically are mediocre,' it is a book which has listened closely to the people it represents and to their culture. *Such Is Life* belies the myth that nineteenth-century Australia was intellectually isolated. Collins describes the Australian landscape as the work of an impressionist artist. Furphy himself bridged that painful and unnecessary gap in Australian history between the life of the mind and manual skill, between education and training. He did things by hand.

It's a pity that neither Furphy's house, nor his shed, are still standing. On the site is a Wilga tree, which Furphy planted, and a plaque. His memory is kept alive in quiet ways.

CHAPTER 23

A River Somewhere

Joseph Conrad, *Heart of Darkness* (1899)

I fell in love with Joseph Conrad (1857–1924) when we studied *Lord Jim* at school. The title, like much in Conrad, is ironic. It is a book about a man who is supposed to be a leader but who, for good reason, lives with crippling self-doubt. It is also, like much in Conrad, about the sea and all who seek their fortune on it.

Joseph Conrad was actually Józef Teodor Konrad Korzeniowski, a name that would have been hard to fit on the cover of a book. He was born in Ukraine of Polish parents; his father's political affiliations meant that his life started in exile. Indeed, exile was where he lived most of his life. English was not his native language, which helps to explain why his writing often ebbs and flows in unexpected ways. You don't splash about in his books. They swell around you like a Mahler symphony. Shortly before he died, Conrad refused a knighthood from the British government. Perhaps he thought his name was long enough already and any further title would only add to the expense of his tombstone. More likely, he thought that titles looked silly on a writer, as petty as a ship on the immensity of the ocean.

I started university in the heyday of what was called postmodernism. One of the tricks of postmodernism is that it won't tell you what it means because meaning itself is a slippery fish that you can serve any way you like. Postmodernism, at least in those days, seemed to embody a belief that you can interpret a work of literature without any reference to the historical circumstances in which it was produced, let alone the people who created it. In this respect, it was exactly the same as biblical fundamentalism, a comparison that neither the fundamentalists nor the postmodernists appreciated. But both groups believed they could take a text and impose their own random sense of order and meaning on it.

I was excited to be starting literature at university in 1984, the year that Orwell had made famous before it even happened. Our first lecture took place in an ageing theatre that accommodated hundreds of impressionable young people and two enormous blackboards. The teacher was a new professor who had arrived with much acclaim in tight jeans and white shoes to shake up what was despised as 'the establishment'. He was the current guru, come to free us all from the ways of old. Those ways had usually involved taking the time to acquire the humility and empathy to understand literature that comes from a different time and place.

The professor's first lecture was on *Heart of Darkness*, Conrad's bijou about the journey of a man in charge of a steamboat creeping up the Congo River into the centre of Africa in search of the mysterious Mr Kurtz, an ivory trader. Mr Kurtz has left his equally mysterious 'intended' behind within the walls of civilisation. At the end of the book, Charlie Marlow, who has narrated the whole story sitting like a 'buddha' or an 'idol' on the deck of a ship, brings news of the death of Kurtz to his intended. She asks what were Kurtz's last words. Marlow, a narrator whose impeccable honesty and honest peccadilloes create the moral core of *Lord Jim*, now lies. 'The last word he pronounced was—your name,' he says.

We never learn the name of Kurtz's intended. She, just as much as the centre of Africa, is uncharted.

This was not good enough for our new professor. He was a postmodernist. What mattered was what he wanted to matter.

He explained that Kurtz was in a French-speaking part of central Africa. His last words are, famously, 'The horror, the horror.' Of course, in French he would have said, 'L'horreur, l'horreur.' This sounds like 'Laura, Laura.' Laura is the heroine of love sonnets written by the fourteenth-century Italian writer Petrarch, who stood at the mouth of the great river of Renaissance humanism. So too did Conrad see himself at the mouth of the great river of modernism and the twentieth century. Obviously, the name of Kurtz's beloved was Laura.

The following week the professor told us that Shakespeare's sonnets are often thought to be dedicated to the 'fair youth' or the 'dark lady'. This, he pontificated, was more traditionalist bullshit. His sonnets are in fact dedicated to black ink, the means, in Marxist terms, by which they were produced.

We had several years in which the arbitrary wit of people like this professor was made to substitute for the wisdom that is required to patiently pass the riches of a culture on to its rightful heirs. We were told that the author was dead. It's a pity that the ego of certain tedious lecturers wasn't dead also.

In Conrad's case, there were endless questions about the nature of European exploitation, a reality that confronts us to this day, no matter how many wisecracks you want to make to stay in the safe zone of playing games. *Heart of Darkness* is based to some extent on a journey Conrad made up the Congo in charge of a steamer in 1890; it draws, too, upon the extraordinary tale of Stanley's search for Livingstone, one of the cornerstone myths of British adventuring in Africa. It asks where the darkness lies. People used to speak about 'deepest, darkest Africa' in a way that sounds patronising. Conrad makes it clear that the darkness is deepest where the power is greatest.

This story, about one river, is told as Marlow sits on a ship on another river, the Thames. 'This also has been one of the dark places of the earth,' he says of the city of London around him. He goes to Brussels to accept his commission, a place described as the 'sepulchral city'. Conrad is shedding light on the darkness that has no heart, the shadows that spread to every corner of the globe. So-called civilisation is as much at the heart of darkness as anywhere else. The Congo River is likened to a snake whose head is the place where the river meets the ocean; it curls back to England, where the book concludes. Marlow meets Kurtz's intended at the end of day, as 'the darkness deepened'. Conrad was indeed writing at the mouth of a violent century. He was looking for meaning, not pissing the idea of meaning up against a wall.

~

Conrad believed that all the rivers and oceans of the world flowed into each other. The Congo is linked to the Thames as much as the Nile is linked to the Hudson or the Yarra, the less-grand river beside the school where I teach. A journey to the heart of darkness can go in either direction. I see this in the stories of students who have come by boat to my small corner of the world.

Timas Harik was one of those. He and I started at the same school on the same day in 2007. Timas was thirteen and just beginning high school. I was a bit older than that, more than thirty years older if we need to put numbers on it. But Timas had travelled further.

Timas was a gifted runner. He was usually running late. For my Year 10 class, he would arrive at the door and explain that he had been detained by some other teacher. This class already included the child of a woman who'd escaped from Vietnam on an unseaworthy boat and had undertaken a courageous journey to get to Australia. There was also the grandchild of people who had barely managed to survive the Cultural Revolution in China; and the great-grandchild of people who had fled the wreckage of Europe after World War II; and at least one boy who told me that he didn't have any background that he was aware of, a form of loss far greater than any of the others. He did, however, get a new phone twice a year. There are some parents who will pay almost anything to impoverish their children.

The room also included a boy whose father had moved away to the other side of the world, another whose father was going through an interminable battle with cancer, another whose twin sister almost died on two occasions as a result of eating disorders, and yet another whose journey to self-acceptance and peace as a person with autism spectrum disorder inspires me even to this day. I don't know why it is called a disorder when, in fact, it can have such a tenacious grasp on order. It's just a different way of experiencing the world.

Every teacher in every school knows what this is like: the wonderful mystery of young lives. We are standing in front of a mosaic whose developing shapes and patterns are hard to categorise.

I don't think Timas understood how much he added to his particular group. He was the one of the first two students in the school to come from Sudan. But he was soon better known because of the numbers that were associated with his name, the improbable times in which he had run certain distances. In Year 7, he had broken school records for various cross-country events known as the poplar run, the rail run and the bridge run. The same occurred again in Year 8.

Indeed, Timas was poetry in motion. He ran with such grace and poise that the time on the scoreboard at the end never described the experience of watching him at work. His head did not rise and fall but sat on an even plane, so much so that in full flight it seemed to balance like a ball on a ridge made by his shoulders. The rest of his body kept that ball in perfect balance on top of his frame. The power seemed to come as much from his chest as his legs; his breathing propelled him. His arms reached out and grabbed the air as though it had handles he could use to pull himself along. His legs seemed the least significant part of the equation.

Like many runners, Timas appeared to walk slowly, to saunter. Perhaps this is why he always arrived a couple of minutes behind the others.

~

As far as he knows, Timas was born on the first day of 1994. The date is a little unsure. The place is not. Khartoum is the capital of Sudan, a country that has since divided from South Sudan. He is a member of the Nubian ethic group and his mother tongue is the Nuba-Moro; twenty years or more later this is the language his family still uses at home. Khartoum, standing at the junction of the Blue Nile and the White Nile, has a niche in the history of Timas's adopted city, Melbourne. We have a small park near the centre of town called Gordon Reserve, boasting statues of the poet Adam Lindsay Gordon and General Charles Gordon, better known as Gordon of Khartoum. Gordon was hailed as a pillar of empire. His fame brought an image of nobility, virtue and fair play at the very moment that Melbourne was starting to get rich from the goldrush. He was supposed to remind people that there was more to life than business. As Conrad well knew, the empire was the biggest piece of real estate in the history of the world.

Charles Gordon was a runner. He went everywhere on foot at breakneck speed, so much so that his subordinates had trouble keeping up with him. That is where the similarities with Timas end. Unlike Livingstone and Stanley, Gordon was religious to the point of obsession. He thought he discovered the location of the Garden of Eden in Mauritius, based on the fact that he found fruit there in the shape of both male and female genitalia, clearly proving that this was the tree of the forbidden fruit. He also located the place where Christ was crucified in Jerusalem and his body was laid. It's not clear what evidence he based this on.

Gordon had a commitment to justice, starting a school for poor kids in Gravesend and being repulsed by the African slave trade. He was eccentric, difficult, a chain-smoker and short, an unlikely flag carrier for the colonial team. It was sad, when he would have preferred to be off looking for Noah's Ark, that history put him on a steamboat on the Nile and pitted him against another religious obsessive in the figure of Muhammad Ahmad, who called himself the Mahdi. This title implied that he was the successor of the prophet, a title not far removed from 'messiah'. The Mahdi disputed British sovereignty in Sudan. He wanted Islamic sovereignty and an end to drinking gin. Gordon, like many of his club, called the place The Sudan, a condescending objectification a bit like The Lebanon or The Ukraine.

Gordon was despatched up the Nile to dislodge the Mahdi. To cut a long story short, he was besieged in Khartoum and was killed there fulfilling his godly duty, soon becoming a cult figure and a Victorian icon. The sun never set on images of Gordon's Last Stand. Tennyson wrote of him:

Thou livest in all hearts, for all men know
This earth hath borne no simpler, nobler man.

Timas Harik travelled the Nile in the opposite direction. His family was forced to leave his country of birth because, as he tells the story, the tension between Islam and Christianity was no better than in Gordon's time, probably worse. Timas's family was Christian. His father, Butros, was a teacher who worked a second job as a cleaner to support his four children, eventually to become five. His mother, Autiya, was an administrative assistant at his father's school and also worked as a cleaner after hours. As a little kid, Timas did not see his parents much. 'They were never there. They worked non-stop just to survive.'

He became self-reliant. He never craved attention. To this day, you never feel Timas has any need to impress you. He doesn't talk big about himself. He doesn't talk much about himself at all.

Young Timas also got used to the fact that there would always be soldiers outside his church and that the names of members of the congregation would be written down.

The Harik family coped with the constant harassment as best they could. Nevertheless, a line was crossed when Timas's grandfather, his dad's dad, was shot in the shoulder by a soldier after church. Kajo had been a preacher and community leader. He survived for a time but died as a result of his injuries and the septicaemia to which they gave rise. He was only in his sixties. The authorities never even bothered to come up with an excuse for what had happened. There was no investigation or court case or pretence of justice. The Harik family knew they were no longer safe in their own country.

Butros and Autiya and their three other sons headed north. Timas was chosen to remain in Khartoum to support his grandmother while she mourned her husband and dealt with their affairs. He was only four.

Eventually, Timas and his grandmother also left. They took a train to a dock on the Nile. This part of the journey took twenty-four hours. Timas remembers a man hiding under his seat the whole time. The train was crowded and the man could not afford a ticket. Even at that age, Timas understood what the man was going through and helped him to remain out of sight.

After the train, Timas and his grandmother spent seven days on a slow boat, the kind of steamer that was in use in Conrad's day. There were no beds and limited seating. They slept where they could find room. It was hot on the deck. Timas remembers making sure his grandmother had water. He wangled it out of the crew; it tasted slightly of diesel.

Finally, the family was reunited in a refugee settlement in Cairo sponsored by the United Nations. Three families— twenty-seven people—shared the same small dwelling. There was no such thing as personal space. Timas learnt how to make that within himself. He also learnt Arabic.

Out of the blue, the Harik family was offered resettlement in Australia under a humanitarian program. Once again, the family headed off first and Timas was left behind. He is not sure of the reasons for this. He was now aged nine. For nine months, he was thrown onto his own resources. The other people in the house kept an eye on him, but he was running his own race.

Finally, on a cold day in December, he was reunited with his family at Melbourne Airport. 'I could never describe what it was like to see my mother again. It was the best day of my life. Mum was crying.'

'Did you cry?'

'Nearly.'

He made it sound like he had almost committed a crime.

The head of his primary school found him a running coach. The coach was an old boy of the school where I was soon to get a job and he rang our headmaster. A connection was made. Timas would travel forty kilometres a day to get to and from school. By his standards, it wasn't far. Running has taken Timas to America, Bahamas and South Korea. He has trained in Kenya alongside David Rudisha, the 2012 Olympic champion. In Kenya, high-altitude training enabled him to improve his lung capacity.

His preferred distance is eight hundred metres. His best time is around 1.47. That's a minute and forty-seven, not an hour and forty-seven. This is a sport in which the tiniest fraction of a second can have the kind of significance it just doesn't have when you are stuck in traffic.

In 2016, he needed 1.45 to be in contention for the Rio Olympics. He was not well during the trials and just missed out. Two seconds may as well have been a week.

'I'm happy,' he said.

~

Timas vividly remembers our class. He used to entertain the others with occasional tales from his adventures working for an infamous fried-chicken franchise in the northern suburbs. Once, a rather large customer ordered a bucket of chicken from the driver's seat of his truck, twelve pieces of greasy flesh that were sold on Tuesdays for a bargain price. The man told Timas through the window that he hoped the chicken would be fresh and not dry or burnt. 'Not like you, Muhammad.'

Timas retaliated by handing the gentleman his twelve greasy pieces, enough calories to last the average person for several days, and a single paper napkin.

The man drove off but then rejoined the queue and a few minutes later appeared at the window again to demand more serviettes.

'I suppose that's your idea of hygiene, sharing napkins,' said the man.

'Oh,' said Timas, cool as a cucumber, casting an eye briefly at the man's stomach. 'I thought you were going to eat the lot yourself.'

The class was in stitches. They were barracking for Timas. That was his gift to the group. He had come on a steamboat along a river as long as history, found our heart of darkness and helped us laugh at it.

CHAPTER 24

Love Came So Lightly

John Shaw Neilson, 'Love's Coming' (1896)

When our children were little, we lived about a kilometre from the place where John Shaw Neilson (1872–1942) is buried, in Melbourne's Footscray cemetery. As places of pilgrimage go, it is hardly Arlington. The cemetery is wedged between two main roads, one of which is the major arterial between the Port of Melbourne and all points west. Thousands of trucks grind their way past every day, loaded with containers full of imported goods. It's just as well that the dead don't speak plain words because you wouldn't have a ghost of a chance of hearing what they were saying.

In the period after my mother died in 2011, I used sometimes to visit Neilson's grave. Mum is buried nine hundred kilometres away and Neilson has always been a poet to whom I have turned in times of trouble. It's strange how often a tough day at work will end with a few minutes in his company. This is because Neilson's poetry can soften the hardest place. He is an alchemist who turns stone into air. His life was one of unremitting physical hardship; his poetry is as ethereal as a gentle breeze on a hot day. Where there is grief, he sows hope.

One time, I was standing in the cemetery and happened to look across to the other main road. It too is a montage of businesses that don't make the tourist brochures, a place so loud with colour that it has become colourless. There are car yards, building suppliers and plumbing warehouses. There was also a funeral parlour two doors from a well-known brothel. It was not well known to me, I hasten to add. In between was a takeaway shop with tables out the front. I observed a gentleman emerge from the brothel, put on his tie as he stopped to talk to a couple of truckies who were eating burgers and chips at the tables outside the greasy spoon, then skip merrily into the funeral parlour. Of course, there is an ageless connection between sex and death but this scenario left me confused.

John Shaw Neilson wrote of experiences that were both more simple and subtle. He will never count for much in a world where both sex and death are matters of commerce.

There is little in Melbourne's inner west to mark the time Neilson spent here in the declining years of his life, from 1928 to 1942, performing the light duties of which he was capable for the Country Roads Board. He was a stranger to the city and didn't much like it, having lived mostly in the western parts of Victoria, but his health had been so devastated by years of back-breaking manual labour that some friends wanted to ease his burden and raised money to help him. He had been unemployed and was in desperate circumstances, as he had been for most of his life. But he didn't write much verse in the city. The house he shared with his sister, Annie, in Gordon Street has been demolished to make way for a hospital car park. There is a bust of him in the Footscray Library, looking out over the hundreds of students from all over the world who study there, taking advantage of educational opportunities that eluded Neilson. He would have been delighted to see young people building new lives in this way; he himself had less than two years of formal schooling. Other than the bust, there isn't much. Yet, whenever I walked past his grave, it appeared that someone had left flowers or a card or a note in an envelope. I am not the only person whom Neilson still touches.

Neilson was born in in 1872 in Penola, a small town in South Australia with an enormous place in the spiritual history of Australia. Mary MacKillop started a school there in a stable. Adam Lindsay Gordon (see Chapter 23) had been a policeman there and one of Neilson's early publications, 'Sheedy Was Dying', is reminiscent of Gordon's 'The Sick Stockrider'. After Adam Lindsay Gordon took his own life, Marcus Clarke wrote a celebrated preface to his poetry. He said:

> In Australia alone is to be found the Grotesque, the Weird, the strange scribblings of Nature learning how to write. Some see no beauty in our trees without shade, our flowers without perfume, our birds who cannot fly, and our beasts who have not yet learned to walk on all fours. But the dweller in the wilderness acknowledges the subtle charm of this fantastic land of monstrosities. He becomes familiar with the beauty of loneliness.

Whispered to by the myriad tongues of the wilderness,
he learns the language of the barren and the uncouth.

There is a great deal about this that could apply to Neilson, a
poet of both loneliness and desolation, one profoundly affected
by the heritage of his landscape. The difference is that Neilson
takes us to much quieter and more tender places than the
galloping tempo of Adam Lindsay Gordon. Gordon was
always on horseback. He sought escape in speed, bravado,
daring, machismo. Neilson was usually on foot. He trudged
from job to job, often distances of 120 kilometres, often short
of water. His poetry celebrates 'Nature learning how to write'.

It also struggles. Neilson's mother, Margaret, was a God-
fearing woman of whom God himself might have been afraid.
Her religion was as hard as the baked earth; she was as controlling as the drought. Neilson was to deal with her legacy in
many poems, not least the exquisite 'The Gentle Water Bird',
dedicated to Mary Gilmore (see Chapter 20). It begins:

In the far days, when every day was long,
Fear was upon me and the fear was strong
Ere I had learned the recompense of song.

In the dim days I trembled for I knew
God was above me, always frowning through,
And God was terrible and thunder-blue.

His father, John, was rather different, but equally problematic.
He was an infernal optimist, dragging young Jock, as Neilson
was known, from one hopeless job to the next. John was impul-
sive, a dreadful planner and a dreamer; but he loved poetry

and that was a lifeline for his son. *The Australian Dictionary of Biography* observes that John Shaw Neilson had more than two hundred different jobs in thirty years. When she finally met him, Mary Gilmore, no stranger to the lives of working men, was appalled: 'When I saw his work-swollen hands, with the finger nails worn to the quick by the abrading stone, I felt a stone in my heart.'

All of this is part of the mystery of Neilson's poetry, much of which is pure angel dust. Take these lines from 'Love's Coming', written in 1896 and finally published in May 1911:

> Quietly as rosebuds
> Talk to thin air,
> Love came so lightly
> I knew not he was there.

Reading this poem in the *Sydney Sun* prompted Mary Gilmore to contact Neilson, and thus began a correspondence in which he found support. He replied to Gilmore: 'I really did not think that anyone should be so affected by my verse…I daresay you can feel things that I cannot feel at all.'

The poem is beautiful for several reasons beyond initiating this important relationship. First of all, Jock's father remarried in March 1911. Margaret had died of 'typhoid and exhaustion' at Christmas, 1897. For all her asperity, she had held the family together. His father's remarriage at the age of sixty-seven was to a woman, Elizabeth, who was forty years his junior. His eldest son, Jock, was never to marry and one biographer speculates that part of the reason was a sense of responsibility to his father's second family in the likely event that his father should die before they reached maturity. Certainly, Jock could never afford to marry. So the masterpiece he published at that time suggests an absence, a longing for love, even an oversight. It is one of the most tender love poems, written by someone who had missed out on romance. Love, in this case, is a 'he'.

The poem is blind. Love is felt and heard, but not seen. It was published in a time when Neilson's eyesight was going from bad to worse. The fine-blown Mallee dust of Victoria's Western Districts had played havoc with his vision, problems that began before he turned twenty. They appear on the third page of his autobiography, finally published almost four decades after his death. By 1911, when his father got married, Neilson took advantage of being in Melbourne to consult oculists, as he called them. He went to three different doctors but none could do very much. The last one did give him glasses, which helped to some extent. 'I could read a little by going out into the open, but writing always seemed to bother me.'

So John Shaw Neilson joined the company of Homer, Milton and Borges, writers whose vision was larger than sight.

~

In 2016, we took a family holiday to Adelaide, driving across the wide open places in western Victoria through which Neilson had trudged. We stopped briefly at Dow Well, a scratch on the map west of Nhill, where there is a memorial to John Shaw Neilson. It remembers the ill-fated farm his family had in the area when his father took up a selection of land, and his younger siblings were able to get some education in a nearby one-room schoolhouse which also employed his sister as a sewing instructor. It was here, in the early 1890s, when Jock was scraping a living from the scornful landscape, that his first poems appeared in the local paper.

After many miles in the car I was glad to step outside, away from the metal shell that had insulated us from the drama of the landscape. It was winter. Within minutes, the wind was toying with me. The space unfolded in every direction. It was immense. I stared, thinking of the backbreaking labour that John Shaw Neilson and his father had needlessly invested in clearing the area of trees. The poet suffered an accident to his thumb that detracted from his already precarious income because he could no longer swing an axe. Part of me wanted to cheer for the trees that may have been saved. But that misunderstands the choices of those who have no choice. I said a few words of thanks that this rugged place had come to find rest in such gossamer poetry.

I turned back to the car, where my three children were glued to their screens. 'How long till we get there?' they asked.

'Perhaps we are there,' I replied.

CHAPTER 25

Unvisited Tombs

George Eliot, *Middlemarch* (1871)

I was relieved when Jenny said it was time for me to propose marriage. I had been wondering about the matter and was glad she brought it up. I can be slow with social clues and if she had told me it was time to put out the garbage I would probably have been equally co-operative.

I had previously been in the Jesuit order for twenty-one years and—without going into connubial details—it was a considerable change. I felt for Jenny. It is not easy to team up with someone whose ex is God. Jenny, as it happens, is a lot easier to fathom than God and hence easier to get along with. God is also slow with social clues, preferring to do things her own way and leave the rest of us to try to figure it out.

I drew comfort from the fact that some of the most horrendous proposals of marriage in the history of literature are delivered by clergy. Perhaps the most famous comes from the insufferable Mr Collins, who wants to take the hand of Elizabeth Bennet in Jane Austen's *Pride and Prejudice* (see Chapter 31):

> My reasons for marrying are, first, that I think it a right thing for every clergyman in easy circumstances (like myself) to set the example of matrimony in his parish. Secondly, that I am convinced it will add very greatly to my happiness; and thirdly, which perhaps I ought to have mentioned earlier, that it is the particular advice and recommendation of the very noble lady whom I have the honour of calling patroness.

No better is the approach St John Rivers makes to Jane Eyre in Charlotte Brontë's novel (see Chapter 29). Rivers, like Collins, is looking for a social accessory and, in this case, cheap labour:

> God and nature intended you for a missionary's wife. It is not personal, but mental endowments they have given you: you are formed for labour, not for love. A missionary's wife you must—shall be. You shall be mine: I claim you—not for my pleasure, but for my Sovereign's service.

But the most devastating comes from Mr Casaubon in the early stages of *Middlemarch* by George Eliot (1819–80). Casaubon is an old fossil of a clergyman who devotes his life to compiling a 'Key to All Mythologies', a dry and lifeless academic project which becomes a place for him to hide from his inability to cope with the world or to form relationships.

If Collins is looking for an accessory and Rivers for cheap labour, Casaubon is looking for a prisoner to share his cell. His target is the orphaned Dorothea Brooke, one of the most painstakingly drawn heroines in nineteenth-century literature.

> My dear Miss Brooke,—I have your guardian's permission to address you on a subject than which I have none more at heart. I am not, I trust, mistaken in the recognition of some deeper correspondence than that of date in the fact that a consciousness of need in my own life had arisen contemporaneously with the possibility of my becoming acquainted with you. For in the first hour of meeting you, I had an impression of your eminent and perhaps exclusive fitness to supply that need…and each succeeding opportunity for observation has given the impression an added depth by convincing me more emphatically of that fitness which I had preconceived, and thus evoking more decisively those affections to which I have but now referred.

The difference between Dorothea Brooke and both Elizabeth Bennet and Jane Eyre is that Dorothea accepts this proposal, despite its obvious selfishness. She takes six terse lines to do so: 'I can look forward to no better happiness than that which would be one with yours.'

George Eliot is a great writer because she takes enormous narrative risks. *Daniel Deronda* (1876), her last novel, is among the first English novels to explore the complexity of the English Jewish community, as opposed to the retailing of shimmering stereotypes in Dickens' *Oliver Twist* (1839).

In *Middlemarch*, Eliot consigns her heroine to a dusty obscurity as early as Chapter 5, which may seem like sabotaging your own book. Most of the other characters (*Middlemarch* has plenty of them) treat news of the engagement a bit like the announcement of an impending death. It takes more than four hundred pages to work through this tangle and finally get Casaubon into his grave.

Yet, in 2015, *Middlemarch* was named in a poll conducted by the BBC as the greatest novel ever written in English. The runners-up included books by many women writers: *Mrs Dalloway* (see Chapter 19), *Jane Eyre* (see Chapter 29) and *Frankenstein* (see Chapter 30). *Middlemarch* is less tightly orchestrated than any of those books. It is a garden in which all sorts of things are allowed to grow, almost unkempt, except they are often fixed with the author's finely written nameplates, telling you exactly what they are. Eliot often interrupts her own book to make astute observations, a player commenting on the game they are taking part in:

> If youth is the season of hope, it is often so only in the sense that our elders are hopeful about us; for no age is so apt as youth to think its emotions, partings and resolves are the last of their kind. Each crisis seems final, simply because it is new.

> Some gentlemen have made an amazing figure in literature by general discontent with the universe as a trap of dullness into which their great souls have fallen by mistake; but the sense of a stupendous self and an insignificant world may have its consolations.

George Eliot thinks with her heart and feels with her mind, skills that make her novels feel complete. *Middlemarch* attempts the total portrayal of a regional community in a time of enormous change, represented by the coming of the railway. The railway was, as many have remarked, the internet of the nineteenth century. It rattles settled communities in novels such as Dickens' *Dombey and Son* (1848; a neglected masterpiece of melodrama in which the railroad is somewhat on the side of the nasty people) and Elizabeth Gaskell's episodic *Cranford* (1853). *Middlemarch* mourns the passing of one way of life but does not condemn the arrival of its replacement. The book is full of contrasts: there are competing approaches to medicine, politics, land ownership and religious ministry. It is an elaborate portrait.

George Eliot was born Mary Ann Evans, often known as Marion Evans, and, when she courted scandal in 1852 by beginning to live openly with a man who was married to someone else and whose wife had children from different fathers, she used his surname. George Henry Lewes, an intellectual and writer, was the love of her life. Both were described euphemistically as 'plain', a judgement that often reflects more on the person making it than anyone else. In Lewes' company, she became M. E. Lewes.

After Lewes died, she married a man twenty years younger than her, John Cross, and became Mrs Cross. Soon after the wedding, Cross tried to kill himself. He survived but she died of renal disease within a few months. Cross later wrote a valuable memoir of his wife. At different times, she also used pet names such Clematis (a flower related to 'mental beauty') and, after she had alienated her dear father by switching from a passionate evangelical Christianity to a considered and tentative atheism, she called herself Apollyon, the name of a destructive angel.

None of these names was George Eliot, the author of novels as intricate as the author's experience of the world. She shed many skins. She was prepared to forfeit a relationship with her brother, Isaac, with whom she was close, in order to live with Lewes. She spent years translating David Friedrich Strauss's turgid fifteen-hundred-page *Life of Jesus*, yet was prepared to leave the safety of a secure Christian home and community to enter more intellectual waters as an editor working on the *Westminster Review*.

I have a copy of *Middlemarch* I found at a jumble sale for one dollar. Inside it is inscribed:

> For Mum, with hopes that you will enjoy this more than the mini-series! I've made a star by the sentence that my Victorian Lit teacher thinks is the best sentence ever written. I do like it too. Love Kez.

There's no knowing if Kez was a son or daughter, but Mary Ann Lewes would have enjoyed this. She may have envied a child able to share literature with a mother; her own mother died when she was seventeen and still in the thrall of an adolescent religiosity, one of the ways the young and insecure can keep people at a safe distance. Sharing literature may have led to something richer and less defensive. More than that, she would have smiled at a young person who repeats what a lecturer has said and then, rather disdainfully, concurs: 'I do like it too.'

The sentence marked in the book is actually two sentences:

If we had a keen vision and feeling of all ordinary
human life, it would be like hearing the grass grow and
the squirrel's heart beat, and we should die of that roar
that lies on the other side of silence. As it is, the quickest
of us walk about well-wadded with stupidity.

I also like them. But neither of these is my favourite sentence
in the book. For me, that sentence is the last one. Indeed,
readers sometimes offer opinions about the best opening line
ever written. But if there was a prize for the last sentence of a
book, *Middlemarch* wins it hands down. It describes Dorothea,
who has at long last married the artist Will Ladislaw, a man
maligned and wronged by his cousin, Mr Casaubon. Ladislaw
is the mirror image of Casaubon and Casaubon was so threat-
ened by the vibrant younger man that he set up his will such
that, if Dorothea ever married Ladislaw, she would lose her
property. This doesn't stop her.

Her second marriage brings almost as much opprobrium
as her first. Dorothea and Ladislaw have a son and finally
Dorothea reaches the end of her days. The book then returns
to a gesture it makes in its prelude and invokes the sixteenth-
century Spanish contemplative Teresa of Ávila. It goes on, in a
vein similar to the sentence Kez approved of above, to celebrate
the small fidelities that create the future far more surely that
great infidelities: 'but we insignificant people with our daily
words and acts are preparing the lives of many Dorotheas.'
Middlemarch concludes:

But the effect of her being on those around her was incalculably diffusive: for the growing good of the world is partly dependent on unhistoric acts; and that things are not so ill with you and me as they might have been, is half owing to the number who lived faithfully a hidden life, and rest in unvisited tombs.

CHAPTER 26

An Old Tree

Leo Tolstoy, *War and Peace* (1869)

At no time in his life would it have been much fun to know the Russian writer Leo Tolstoy (1828–1910).

As a young man, Tolstoy was a gambler and a womaniser, riddled with insecurity and unable to control his impulses. As a middle-aged man, he made preposterous demands on his wife, Sonya, who married him when she was sixteen and he was thirty-six. Those demands started at the time of their wedding when, with characteristic insensitivity, he required her to read the diaries which detailed his previous relationships. With further insensitivity, he turned this incident into fodder for the characterisation of Levin in *Anna Karenina* (1877). Tolstoy never fully recognised the debt he owed Sonya, with whom he had thirteen children, insisting that she give birth on the same battered leather couch on which they had been conceived.

He was a man of almost bestial appetites: his diet included curdled horse milk. He was an aristocrat who wanted to live like a serf. But he could never think like a serf. As an old man, he elevated himself above the common herd of humanity and became a kind of guru; many of the writings of that period dealing with non-violence, justice and the crisis of faith inspired the likes of Gandhi and Martin Luther-King. In *Long Walk to Freedom* (see Chapter 9), Nelson Mandela pays tribute to the effect on him of *War and Peace* while he was incarcerated for decades. Tolstoy wrote wonderfully about compassion. He wasn't nearly as good at practising it. My sympathies are nearly always with Sonya. If she had not painstakingly copied his manuscripts, Tolstoy's great novels would have remained a sheaf of illegible scrawl.

For all that, I owe to Tolstoy a greater debt than to possibly any other writer. Tolstoy understood the difference between pleasantness and happiness.

I will never forget the Saturday night in 1974 when we were all taken into Sydney Hospital to say our final goodbyes to Dad, who was expected to die that night from renal failure. I was twelve. We had just taken delivery of a colour TV, the latest technological advance. We arrived home in a sorry state and put it on as a distraction. The first episode of the BBC's production of *War and Peace* began and instantly I was hooked. I had never heard of *War and Peace*. It was a terrific story and, best of all, it had nothing whatever to do with my life at that point. It is set two hundred years ago in Russia and is full of costumes and banquets, at least at the start. The BBC production features a young Anthony Hopkins. He plays the part of

Pierre Bezukhov, the illegitimate son of a great count who, in the opening episode, is about to die. Through the machinations of an aunt, Pierre is made legitimate and inherits an enormous fortune. He embarks on a pleasant but desperately unhappy life.

I started reading *War and Peace* in sync with each week's episode. I still have my tie-in copy with all my adolescent underlinings as well as countless bits of coloured paper on which I have dutifully written out quotes that struck me as worthy of my attention, such as 'we must believe in the possibility of happiness in order to be happy' and 'youth is no bar to courage.' It is a long book, about fourteen hundred pages, but a page-turner. Somebody called it the greatest work of pulp fiction ever written.

War and Peace follows Pierre Bezukhov in his search for meaning. He tries everything. He has an unhappy marriage, gambles, fights a duel, dabbles with freemasonry and considers the army. Indeed, when Pierre goes through initiation as a freemason, being confronted by such images as a skull, a coffin and a burning candle, he is disappointed because they are not extreme enough. Pierre was 'hoping to enter a new life absolutely removed from the old one'.

Meanwhile, Russia is being invaded by the Napoleonic forces. Everyone flees Moscow ahead of the conquerors, and Pierre is left wandering alone in his two enormous and very pleasant mansions. He is taken prisoner and narrowly escapes the firing squad. For the first time in his life, he is among peasants and has no idea of how to look after himself.

Luckily, he is befriended by one of my favourite characters in literature, Platon Karataev, a wily peasant with a fund of wise sayings. Platon asks God to lie him down like a stone every night and in the morning raise him up like new bread. That is a great approach to life. Platon takes Pierre under his wing, which is just as well because the Cossacks are moving the prisoners through the snow at a remorseless pace and anyone who can't keep up is taken to the side of the column, shot and left for dead. Without Platon's help, this would have happened to Pierre. Tolstoy was developing a philosophy that it is the so-called little people, those like Platon, who are the architects of history more than those with famous names.

~

Then comes the time when Platon gets sick and he can't keep up. The Cossacks take him aside and shoot him. What follows is a line buried on about page eleven hundred of a huge dog-eared paperback that changed my life. The line says that when Platon is shot, Pierre doesn't even look back. I have been literally winded by a book on only a small number of occasions. One was when I first read the last line of Orwell's *Nineteen Eighty-Four*, 'He loved Big Brother.' Another was in Year 12 when we were reading Dickens' *Great Expectations* and Pip realises what he has done to his gentle mentor, Joe Gargery. Seeing the way Pierre Bezukhov trashed his dear friend has stayed with me for forty years.

That moment is the beginning of Pierre's rebirth. He came to realise that he was capable of as much evil as Napoleon or the Cossacks or anyone else. He touched the bedrock of his humanity and found it bare. But once he had owned the truth of himself he was able to begin again and to build. He discovered his own need for forgiveness and healing. This was the start of happiness. There was nothing pleasant about it.

What started for me as escapism brought me back to reality by another door. This has been the greatest gift of reading to me.

~

Earlier in the novel, another troubled character, Andrei Bolkonsky, is returning to his family estate after his first experience of war. He is shattered. At the gate, he sees a grumpy old oak tree, refusing, it seems, to join the rites of spring. The tree reminds him of himself:

> With huge ungainly limbs sprawling unsymmetrically, with gnarled hands and fingers, it stood, an aged monster, angry and scornful, among the smiling birch-trees. The oak alone refused to yield to the season's spell, spurning both spring and sunshine.

But as he leaves a few days afterwards, he notices that even this angry and bitter tree has been brought back to life:

> The old oak, quite transfigured, spread out a canopy of dark, sappy green, and seemed to swoon and sway in the rays of the evening sun. There was nothing now to be seen of knotted fingers and scars, of old doubts and sorrows. Through the rough, century-old bark, even where there were no twigs, leaves had sprouted, so juicy, so young that it was hard to believe that aged veteran had borne them.
>
> 'Yes, it is the same oak,' thought Prince Andrei, and all at once he was seized by an irrational, spring-like feeling of joy and renewal.

~

Thirty years later, Tolstoy was to compress many of the most powerful insights of *War and Peace* into the slim novella *The Death of Ivan Ilyich* (1886), a work I have loved sharing with students. Tolstoy had learnt the philosopher's art of condensation and distillation, a painful art to practise. *The Death of Ivan Ilyich* is wonderful in its simplicity.

The main character has a pleasant life. A decent life, you might say. But that is a far thing from a happy life. Yet he ends up having a happy death. Tolstoy believes that a happy anything, even death, is better than a pleasant anything, even life. Pleasantness is about matching someone else's ideas, measuring your life by what might be in fashion. Happiness is about freedom, and this includes freedom from the tyranny of pleasing, especially the tyranny of pleasing yourself.

Tolstoy lived into his eighties, so he had a long time to think about things. He believed with good cause that all happiness lay in finding freedom from the ego. His own life proved the point. He was an egomaniac and, for the most part, desperately unhappy.

One of my life's ambitions is to visit the Tolstoy estate at Yasnaya Polyana, about two hundred kilometres south of Moscow. It has little in common with the world in which I live. Yet what happened there has enriched me enormously. I am just quietly happy that I won't be required to meet Count Tolstoy when I get there.

CHAPTER 27

The Commander of an Army

Isabella Beeton, *Mrs Beeton's Book
of Household Management* (1861)

There is an honourable place for junk food in the history of
literature. You might think of Achilles' souvlaki in *The Iliad*
(see Chapter 38) or the Franklin's meat pies in Chaucer's *The
Canterbury Tales* (see Chapter 35). John Kennedy Toole's glorious
comedy of bad manners *A Confederacy of Dunces* (1980) is espe-
cially high on saturated fats and processed gluten. Dickens'
Nicholas Nickleby (1839) starts with an appalling man of business,
Ralph Nickleby, attempting to become the prototype of Colonel
Sanders by investing in the United Metropolitan Improved Hot
Muffin and Crumpet Baking and Punctual Delivery Company.

I confess that I think of a cookbook as something to read
while you wait for the pizza to be delivered. Luckily, the mother
of the genre, *Mrs Beeton's Book of Household Management*, has
an eye out for me. Mrs Beeton is ever practical. She says that

macaroons are too much bother to cook. Go and buy them. Same with turtle soup, which is best purchased in tins.

Aside from that, she has eighteen hundred recipes, nearly all pilfered from other sources, for you to deploy. Her stockpile of culinary and other advice, plundered from wherever she could find it, is an arsenal to use against every conceivable domestic challenge. She sets out by describing the mistress of the house as 'the commander of an army'. Her tone doesn't deviate from that pitch, especially when she is railing against her pet hates, which include apples, potatoes, tomatoes and a shortage of servants.

~

I don't like the word 'recipe'. Those of us who picked up a smattering of Latin at school may recall that the word is a verb. It is an imperative meaning 'take'. It gained currency because the first word of any recipe was always 'take'. *Take two eggs, a cup of water and something else.* The same word was used in dispensing, a reminder that cooking is, after all, a form of chemistry. *Take two tablets, a cup of water and something else.* My problem with this innocent little word is that what we call a recipe is not an imperative at all. It is an invitation. An invitation is a question. A recipe wants to pass on a lot of experience, but it also asks you to find your own way, to do it yourself. This is why I find Mrs Beeton's imperious manner a source of grim amusement.

One of the most inviting recipes I know comes from a small book my mother picked up when she was paying her gas bill in the 1940s. Our kitchen was just about the smallest room in the house. It was Mum's place but it belonged to us all as her invited guests. We practically lived in it, especially in winter when Mum would light the gas oven and leave its door open to heat the room. We had to sit in front of the oven to dry our hair. When that was done, our towels would be hung in front of it. Mum hated the cold. She waged a defensive war against it, so much so that I am the only person I know who thinks of Sydney, where I grew up, as a cold place. Mum curtly told anybody who left the kitchen door ajar to put the board in the hole. On cold mornings she would put our shoes in the oven to warm them before we went to school. I'm sure I thought that the oven was an item of laundry equipment. After all, Mum's twin-tub washing machine nestled nearby. Most of the serious cooking happened in the electric frypan.

In our house, the kitchen was both the laundry and the phone room. We ate at the kitchen table, usually in shifts. Dad first, then the three kids, then finally Mum. There was a shelf over the table, just above head height, where one of Dad's radios sat. He would emerge on the hour from some other part of the house to listen to the news. The kitchen was also the first-aid centre and the court of arbitration. It was the place where secrets were laid bare.

It was also the place where things could be kept hidden. There were plenty of cupboards for that. Every year, Mum would turn the cupboards inside out. This would invariably lead to the discovery of precious objects that had either been lost or impounded in the previous twelve months. It also led to the bringing forth of items with stories attached, and those stories would be told. There was an enamel pie dish that Mum's dad had used, scone cutters he had made for Mum's mum, a carving fork from Dad's childhood home, items Mum had been given for her shower tea or her wedding—events which seemed unimaginably distant both in time and space. There were items of family significance kept behind glass in the living room, but the kitchen was the real family museum. We never knew Grandad, but we used his breadboard all the time. Mum only made stuffing according to her father's recipe. He was still part of the family.

Perhaps it was lucky that neither of my parents believed in such an idea as a new kitchen. I realised this some years later when I was teaching a difficult fifteen-year-old boy. His form master was invited to his family house for dinner, a state-of-the-art mansion on Sydney's North Shore. The teacher said he came home feeling sorry for the boy for the first time. I asked why. He said that the kid was growing up in a house where the only thing older than him were his parents. In our house we had takeaway food containers, washed out and neatly stacked, that were older than us.

Our meal of the week was Sunday lunch, which we ate about the time people now have brunch. We'd come home from church and Dad, never a well man, would put on the television to watch sports commentary from men in flashy shirts until it was time for a procedure known as 'sitting up at the table': Sunday was the only time we ate at the dining table and Sunday lunch was a tutorial in certain aspects of life. We learnt about the correct arrangement of cutlery and where to place the cruets—the salt, pepper and mustard. These days, children learn much more about *what* to eat: the basic food groups, the need for so many vegetables, the superiority of anything 'organic'. In our day, the emphasis was far more on *how* to eat:

gravy boats, fish knives, butter knives and salt spoons were as much the focus of dining as intolerances and photos are now. Even eating together has become individualised.

If we were lucky, the baked dinner was followed by one of Mum's gingerbread puddings. It was produced in an old pudding bowl, bound up in brown paper and string. The bowl had come from her parents' house.

As an adult, I asked Mum to dig out the recipe for her ginger pudding. I discovered that one of my strongest childhood memories was occasioned by a single line at the end of what was actually a recipe for gingerbread in a promotional giveaway: 'Half of this mixture, steamed for one and a half to two hours, also makes one excellent ginger pudding.' Mum had produced a dilapidated booklet she'd acquired from the North Shore Gas Company long before she was married. It had been hidden in a kitchen cupboard. It was falling apart by now, but you could still read the advertisements for a gas-operated refrigerator (another marvel of modern science) and for a product called Mum's Baking Powder (made with the finest English cream of tartar). This advertisement says:

> When dad and the boys tell mum what wonderful cakes and scones she has made, she has every reason to be proud. Such praise makes up for the work and thought which are every bit as necessary as the other ingredients in good cooking.

My mother was also a working pharmacist. She knew that praise didn't pay the bills.

~

Sam believed in boy's own adventures for himself. Soon after they were married, he passed syphilis on to his wife. This led to the death in infancy of their first child, Sam. The next child survived and was also called Sam. A man who is happy to play round and then name not one but two sons after himself is harder to stomach than his wife's turnip broth.

It was Sam who came up with the idea of the *Book of Household Management*, which first appeared in forty-eight monthly instalments. There had been numerous comprehensive cookbooks before it and Isabella borrowed, to put it politely, liberally from them. She plagiarised material from Alexis Soyer, the legendary cook of the Reform Club who tried to feed the poor of Ireland and went to Crimea to help Florence Nightingale cook for the suffering troops. Come to think of it, she borrowed from Florence Nightingale as well. Much of her medical advice is taken word for word from Miss Nightingale's *Notes on Nursing* (1859).

The public loved her life-coaching skills: 'Friendships should not be hastily formed nor the heart given, at once, to every new-comer.' Modern cookbooks tend to focus on food. Mrs Beeton focusses on everything. She paints a picture of a world in order and under control. Every recipe has not just ingredients but a price as well. Mrs Beeton's magisterial tome often sat in middle-class houses beside the Bible. Indeed, her work was often referred to as a bible, the function it came to fill. There are, of course, recipes in the Bible. And Mrs Beeton has hundreds of commandments.

CHAPTER 28

Ego Dismasted

Herman Melville, *Moby-Dick* (1851)

For twenty years towards the end of his life, Herman Melville (1819–91), a resident of New York, was stuck in a desperately boring job working for the Custom Service. Every day, he caught a tram down Broadway and then walked along the docks on the Hudson River to reach an office (really a draughty shed) that he shared with other wage slaves, people whose tedious work was sometimes compensated by the bribes they were able to take from importers.

Melville does not seem to have resorted to such dishonesty. His duties involved making endless inventories of goods that had come to the country by sea, the small trophies of America's expanding consumerism. Melville was required to check that correct duties had been paid. From the time he started, in 1866, he almost always wore the same clothes, turning up punctually each morning in a coat resembling that of a naval captain.

The scenario is a sad parody of the turbulent relationship with the sea and everything on it that Melville had explored in *Moby-Dick*, one of the most energetic and unruly novels ever written. *Moby-Dick* is a raw study of nature in conflict with itself: it is the story of the obsessive hunt by Ahab, captain of the *Pequod*, for revenge on the great white whale that on a previous voyage humiliated him and cost his leg. 'It was Moby-Dick that dismasted me; Moby-Dick that brought me to this dead stump I stand on now,' cries Ahab to his crew in one of many passages that suggest that the ship and its captain have melded into one being. Ahab has a hole drilled in the deck so he can secure his wooden leg, a bit like a café umbrella, and not be dislodged by the elements. He is the spiritual godfather of the overblown despots who turned modern history into a bloodbath.

The novel is itself no stranger to blood: it is a relic of a time, before the invention of the harpoon cannon, when whaling was hand-to-hand combat, every bit as gruesome as a bayonet charge. This is not to suggest that whaling was later sanitised. Tim Winton (see Chapter 4) has written memorably of witnessing as a child the physical horror of whaling in the West Australian town of Albany as late as the 1960s.

Melville is enthralled by the monster of Ahab's ego, a creature as frightening as the great white whale. Ahab seduces his crew with a mixture of fear, mysticism and intoxicating vision. But everything is focussed on him. He can't cope with anything he can't control. The whale is beyond his grasp. Ahab is not just the prototype of Hitler and Stalin and Mao and Imelda Marcos and a good number of other destructive individuals, far too many to list. He is also the prototype of everyone who can't let go of an injury, no matter what agony that means inflicting on the world and others. It is curious that Ahab's mate Starbuck has given his name to a coffee chain whose range of standardised products is more reminiscent of the custom house than the ocean. But Starbuck is the accessory of every tyrant: the helpful, efficient, compliant and presentable deputy.

Ahab's name, like so much else in *Moby-Dick*, is biblical. It was the name of one of the kings of Israel, a man who could not stick to the law but had to make himself the big boss. The novel's narrator, Ishmael, who is entranced into joining the crew, gets his name from the founder of the Arabic race, the illegitimate child who Abraham had with the slave girl Hagar. Melville invests enormous resources in the spiritual explorations of *Moby-Dick*. He does not do this as some kind of Christian apologist. On the contrary, *Moby-Dick* gets its colossal power largely from the ambivalence Melville felt about absolutely everything, including God, the world and the capacity of the rational mind. He constantly rocks back and forth between belief and despair: 'Though in many of its aspects this visible world seems formed in love, the invisible spheres were formed in fright.'

One of the few close friends Melville made was the writer Nathaniel Hawthorne. Shortly before Hawthorne died, in 1856, Melville visited him in England. One of the last entries Hawthorne made in his journal was about his old friend and sparring partner. He said that Melville:

will never rest until he gets hold of a definite belief. It is strange how he persists—and has persisted ever since I knew him. And probably long before—in wandering to and from over these deserts, as dismal and monotonous as the sand hills amid which we were sitting. He can neither believe nor be comfortable in his unbelief.

The phrase 'he can neither believe nor be comfortable in his unbelief' describes many people. Melville is a wonderful resource for anyone unable to find a simple way to live in a complex world.

Melville married Lizzie Shaw and the couple had four children. We don't get too many glimpses of this relationship but what we do see suggests that it was far from plain sailing. Anyone who has encountered the delicious homoeroticism of many parts of *Moby-Dick*, especially the scene in which Ishmael shares a room with the islander Queequeg, will feel a pang of bafflement on the couple's behalf.

Moby-Dick is full of extraordinary detail about whales and ships and the ocean, material that could have been made to read like inventories for Melville's last paid job. The novel is also febrile and obsessive. There is no shallow water in it and no safe harbour. It takes the reader to unsafe places in every sense of the word. It is a work whose sexuality, spirituality, psychology and philosophy are all untamed. *Moby-Dick* was published in 1851. By 1866, Melville was marooned on shore in the custom house, a place where the traffic of the ocean is reduced to lists of numbers, where every debt has a value in dollars and cents. What happened?

In some ways, Melville was ransacked by his own genius. He was never the same after *Moby-Dick* appeared. It was a book that tore the façade off every pretence in the world, including those Melville needed to preserve his own wellbeing. Nearly all the great works of literature deal with the smallness of being human. But *Moby-Dick* makes a banquet of this theme. It is at war with the human ego.

Melville had plenty of experience of being small. His early books, *Typee* and *Omoo*, were rollicking tales of the Pacific with an erotic tinge, and sold reasonably well. *Moby-Dick* was a bad career move. It did a belly flop, so much so that when most of the first edition was burnt in a warehouse fire at the publisher's, there was not much fuss. Not any, in fact.

Melville's personal life was likewise an experience of being a feather on an ocean. His father went bankrupt when Melville was a child, an event which always made Melville sceptical about the American myth of prosperity. His eldest son, Malcolm, a veteran of the Civil War who wore his uniform even in peacetime, committed suicide with a revolver and was discovered dead upstairs in the family home. His second son, Stanwix, died alone in a hotel room in San Francisco on the other side of the country. And on it went. The man trudging to work was like an Old Testament prophet. He had seen too much. He had dared to speak of what he saw. Those lists of imported goods were nothing like the language he knew was needed to account for reality.

He did labour unsuccessfully at poetry during the evenings after he came home from the office. Then, suddenly, after twenty years, the clouds cleared and Melville wrote *Billy Budd*, a late-life masterpiece not published until 1924. *Billy Budd* is again about tyranny and deceit. But it has an existential clarity. It still doesn't trust the human ego, yet it charts a return to innocence. Like Tolstoy's *The Death of Ivan Ilyich* (see Chapter 26), it is a conscious act of letting go by an old writer who once had much to say but who now chooses to celebrate the possibilities of a final scene. Closure is a silly idea, useful for shop trading hours but not for dealing with grief or loss. *Billy Budd* grieves for the innocent and abused young man at its heart. It needs openness, not closure, in order to do so.

CHAPTER 29

Reader, I Married the Wrong One

Charlotte Brontë, *Jane Eyre* (1847)

There are people who have read *Jane Eyre* a dozen times or more. Then they read it again and find things lurking in its shadows that they never noticed before. It was written at breakneck speed after the first novel, *The Professor*, by Currer Bell, the pen name of Charlotte Brontë (1816–55), had experienced numerous rejections. One publisher suggested it might be willing to look at something else if the author, assumed to be a man, had anything to offer. So most of *Jane Eyre* fell off a scratchy pen, with many ink blots, in matter of weeks. But all the Brontës wrote fast, even Branwell, the brother of the three famous sisters, Charlotte, Emily and Anne. He made a start on a novel during a break in the fog of alcoholic and compulsive behaviour that controlled his short and lovelorn life. They all had short lives, even those who, unlike Branwell, didn't stray far from the straight and narrow. They didn't have time to waste.

The Brontës wrote books that already seem to have one foot in another world: Emily's *Wuthering Heights* (1847) is replete with the spirits of the deceased, Charlotte's *Villette* (1853) features supernatural encounters, and *Jane Eyre* includes an offbeat scene in which the heroine seems to hear Mr Rochester calling her name in some ethereal way to return to him across the miles rather than end up with the dreadful St John Rivers (see Chapter 25). The book ends with the same words as the Bible: 'Come, Lord Jesus.' If you have to plagiarise an author, why not go to the top?

On a recent encounter with *Jane Eyre*, I noticed for the first time how often it uses the word 'terror'. It is one of the most loaded words in the world today: perhaps this is why it lunged for my attention. Jane, the orphan of a poor clergyman whose long-lost relations will eventually have an effect on the story, is consigned to the care of cousins who despise and degrade her. She describes herself as they see her:

> A heterogeneous thing, opposed to them in tempera-
> ment, in capacity, in propensities; a useless thing,
> incapable of serving their interest, or adding to their
> pleasure; a noxious thing, cherishing the germs of
> indignation at their treatment, of contempt of their
> judgement.

The passage is rich in vocabulary, as is every corner of the novel, but the strongest word is 'thing'. Jane is not even allowed the dignity of being a person. In the best of all possible worlds, this might have created a bridge of feeling to the first Mrs Rochester, Bertha, the so-called madwoman in the attic whose survival prevents Jane's marriage to Rochester, at least for a while. Bertha is referred to as an 'it'. Her character stands in contrast to the frugal sanity and moral clarity of Jane Eyre herself. Both Rochester's wives are objectified; it's a pity that two marginalised women need to be rivals. One critic has even spoken of them as two sides of the one person.

Bertha breaks free from the guard of the incompetent Grace Poole, who is paid handsomely to keep her confined but is prone to drink; she lights a couple of celebrated fires. Jane Eyre breaks free from fear. As a girl, she is bullied as a child by John Reed, described as a tyrant who creates 'terror'. She is likewise terrorised at Lowood School, but not to the same extent as the angelic Helen Burns, whose pure saintliness is opposed to the brutality of the reverend Mr Brocklehurst. Charlotte Brontë knew clergymen. Her father, Patrick, was one and she resigned herself to a sensible marriage with another, despite the fact that her heart was inclined elsewhere. She knew that religion could be exploited as battleground of fear.

Finally, Mr Rochester expects Jane to be afraid of him:

'You are afraid of me, because I talk like a sphynx.'
    'Your language is enigmatical, sir: but though I am bewildered, I am certainly not afraid.'
    'You *are* afraid—your self-love dreads a blunder.'

Jane Eyre, both the character and the book, stare down fear. It strengthens the reader. By the end of the novel, when Jane returns to Rochester after a second fire (in which it is possible he has murdered Bertha), he is blind and has lost an arm. Jane, on the other hand, has well and truly found her voice.

~

In the 1840s, the years in which *Wuthering Heights* and *Jane Eyre* were written, the Brontës lived a monastic kind of existence at Haworth, in Yorkshire. In her account of the life of Charlotte Brontë, Elizabeth Gaskell writes as a friend. She has one line that speaks volumes. 'Her life at Haworth was so unvaried that the postman's call was the event of her day.' The coming of the penny post in 1840 changed the lives of the Brontës, especially Charlotte. There survive 350 of her letters to Ellen Nussey, her closest friend and, according to Deborah Lutz, possibly lover. Those letters came to take centre stage in Gaskell's biography.

I admire in the Brontës something that feels like the imagination fighting free. Anyone who has read *Jane Eyre* or *Wuthering Heights* will recognise the sheer force with which the prose breaks out of bonds. Gaskell sums up the pressure that Charlotte lived under in another memorable line: 'She must not hide her gift in a napkin...In an humble and faithful spirit must she labour to do what is not impossible, or God would not have set her to do it.'

In other words, she could not let her talent be caged by the grim circumstances in which she lived. Consider what 1847–48 was like for Charlotte Brontë. Her brother, Branwell, died from consumption in September 1847, aged thirty-one; Emily, her sister, got the bug at his funeral and died at Christmas, aged thirty; Anne, her other sister, joined them the following May, aged twenty-nine. Charlotte survived and became the gatekeeper of the family story, though she had never really understood either the private Emily or the devout Anne. Charlotte received a negative review of *Jane Eyre* in the post within a couple of weeks of burying Emily. Gaskell writes feelingly, 'She was numbed to all petty annoyances by the grand severity of Death.'

Death is spelt with a capital D. It was a character in their lives; it was a family member in every house in Haworth. As the village turned from agriculture to light industry, the population grew out of all proportion to the sewerage and water systems. By the 1850s, the average life expectancy was twenty-five; the infant mortality rate was 41 per cent. The cemetery filled. Charlotte once told Gaskell that she knew 'her death would be quite lonely; having no friend or relation in the world to nurse her and her father dreading a sick room above all places'. Gaskell said that Charlotte 'works off a great deal that is morbid into her writing and out of her life'.

Many years ago, I toured Brontë country with my mother. On a warm summer's afternoon, the narrow winding streets of Haworth seemed anything but death traps. They throbbed with life. Mum and I walked slowly from the railway station up to the parsonage, a bit of a haul. Only when we got to the top did we discover that the land on one side of the parsonage has been given over to an enormous car park, so we could have saved ourselves the effort. On the other hand, *Wuthering Heights* loses something if you try to imagine Heathcliff and Cathy running towards each other across crowded bitumen, especially if their plaintiff voices are lost in the gutturals of buses warming up.

This was once a lonely place; now we queued to get in and follow a carefully mapped route through the house, which prevented congestion by making sure that nobody redoubled their steps. Finally, as always, we made it to the souvenir shop. Here you could buy copies of any of the main Brontë books for a quid, the cost of two postcards. But the postcards were selling a lot better. You could also buy videos: the unfortunate staff worked all day, every day with the 1939 film of *Wuthering Heights* starring Sir Laurence Olivier as Heathcliff running continually in the background. A complete screening will fit comfortably more than twenty times into a regular working week. I hoped the staff was getting a stress loading.

In spite of this, the parsonage stopped us short. Inside the front door is Mr Brontë's study. He was a self-made man, a strange concept for a man of God, having climbed the ladder from Irish beginnings to graduation from Cambridge. Along the way, he upgraded his name from Brunty to Brontë, complete with a sophisticated umlaut. He took his meals on his own in here and could only read the psalms with the aid of a magnifying glass owing to cataracts. On the other side of a narrow corridor, his three daughters circled their working table until late in the night, reading to each other what they had written. Brontë, the parson, perplexes. Any man who, in spite of his blindness, takes a loaded pistol to bed every night and discharges the bullet out his window the following morning makes me nervous.

Thousands visit the parsonage but only a fraction of them seem to make it over to the church where Mr Brontë, unable to look at any clock, preached every week punctiliously for half an hour. He knew when to stop. Actually, half an hour sounds like a pretty good innings in the pulpit, so perhaps he didn't know when to stop. I was lucky in my days as a priest to get away with five minutes.

I looked around the church as if it, too, were an extension of the museum until I found a simple prayer tree at the back. Here the local congregation write down the names of those who need help: the sick, the sad and the sour. They aren't entrusted to any patron saint but merely to the prayers of a community, which is invisible among so many day visitors but evidently still alive. I noticed some girls reading the prayer tree. They had annoyed me in the museum because they kept asking if they could try on all the Brontës' dresses, then giggling when they were told they couldn't.

The girls had inadvertently touched a raw nerve. The Brontës all seem to have been about a size six. One modern biographer believes that Emily had anorexia nervosa. Once the girls had left, I went over to the prayer tree because I assumed they were going to vandalise it. They had written down the name of a thirteen-year-old friend back home who was waiting anxiously for a bone-marrow transplant. They asked the local parish for their prayers.

Something similar happened to us in Stratford-on-Avon. When we went to look for his tomb, we realised that Shakespeare had retired from the theatre and spent some years as a lay minister in the parish close to where he grew up. If the thought of Shakespeare as a young lad sitting in a classroom is enough to threaten any teacher worth their salt, imagine coming to church and hearing Shakespeare read from a Bible in the language to which he added so much colour and flexibility. The Bible he used is still on the stand.

But at the back of Shakespeare's church are the rather gauche creations of 'the Sunday club'. One of them asks you if you can 'find the lost sheep': you look under little paper flaps and see first a cat, then a mouse and finally the sheep. In the ubiquitous gift shop, selling the ubiquitous pencil sharpeners and erasers, a volunteer attendant told the woman behind the counter that somebody from the area had just been taken to hospital. He said over and over that 'It sounds serious.' There is hardly the subtlety of Shakespeare in that sibilance, but save for the fact that ordinary people say ordinary things, Shakespeare would never have been able to say anything special. He would have had nothing to write about and nobody to understand him.

As we were leaving the church in Haworth, a middle-aged woman appeared with her elderly mother on her arm. The mother was blind.

'This must be Catholic,' said the old woman loudly. 'It smells Catholic. Don't you think it smells Catholic?'

The entire graveyard outside turned in one movement.

~

In fact, in the days when such divisions meant more than they did now, Charlotte Brontë did get emotionally involved with a Catholic, Constantin Héger, who ran a boarding school where she worked for a short time in Brussels. She considered Catholicism but found the idea of it too confining: *Villette* explores this, and finds Catholicism both fascinating and repulsive. Anyway, Héger was already married with several children and more on the way. The relationship between him; his wife, Zoë; and Charlotte became complicated. Eventually, Charlotte—having refused several offers of marriage over the years, including one from Ellen Nussey's brother—wed her father's curate, the penniless and unexciting Arthur Nicholls, and died of exhaustion and dehydration during her first pregnancy not long afterwards. She was only thirty-nine but had outlived her siblings. History attests that Ellen Nussey found the marriage very difficult. She seems to have thought that Charlotte had married the wrong one.

It is hard to imagine Jane Eyre choosing the same narrow path. When *Jane Eyre* became a success, Charlotte Brontë was appreciative of the support of critics such as George Lewes, the man who would afterwards become the life partner of George Eliot (see Chapter 25). She wrote to Lewes: 'Out of obscurity I came, to obscurity I can easily return.' It is sad if she believed this. Few of her readers have.

CHAPTER 30

Lonely Creature

Mary Shelley, *Frankenstein* (1818)

On a winter's day in January, our family huddled inside a warm church in North London. We were running late and seated towards the back. This suited our three teenage children, who had reached the stage of life where they so much wanted to be invisible that they drew attention to themselves.

'How long are they going to be married for?' asked my fourteen-year-old son. I think he meant to ask how long the service would take.

We had returned from Rome the night before, so we were tired. My wife had been part of this colourful community twenty years previously and it has remained a mooring point in her life. Bernini had built the colonnade of St Peter's Square in Rome, which we had visited during the week, to express a welcome to the whole world. This place did it without so much fuss. On the way in, a gentleman introduced me to his husband.

Now we were celebrating the wedding of a young woman whom Jenny had looked after as a toddler what seemed like a fortnight ago. Grace had been working among women who struggled with every kind of challenge. She was a person with a strong and gentle sense of where she stood in the world. Today she was standing beside Harry, a superb performance poet. His extraordinary feats of comic verbal dexterity had attracted over two million views of one of his appearances on YouTube. Yet today his voice fell apart when he came to say a few ancient words of promise, words as familiar as they are awesome. 'For richer and for poorer, in sickness and in health.' They are words of giving and surrender; Harry was present in them, not performing them.

When Harry's voice cracked, I started to blubber, earning me a swift dig in the ribs from my embarrassed fourteen-year-old. But Harry's words had liberated me from all the hassles of the moment and I grabbed Jenny's hand, full of gratitude, even for impatient children, especially for her hand. The archdeacon, Liz, reminded us of the power of community. A marriage involves far more than two people. This celebration was all about substance, not image. How could I keep from crying? Afterwards, we had baklava and peppermint tea. Jacob, my younger son, looked at my wedding ring as if he had never seen it before; the finger had grown around it.

'Can you get this off?' he asked.

'It wouldn't be easy,' I said.

~

The following day, Sunday, I went to find the place where Mary Godwin (1797–1851) had married the poet Percy Bysshe Shelley (1792–1822), a few days after Christmas in 1816. They had chosen the church of St Mildred's, designed by Christopher Wren, in Bread Street, because this was the narrow thoroughfare in Cheapside where the poet John Milton was born in 1608. It is a stone's throw from Wren's masterpiece, St Paul's Cathedral.

Mary married an atheist and was the daughter of an atheist philosopher, William Godwin. Atheists were harder to come across in those days and she found two. Yet she also had an intense relationship with Milton's epic creation story, *Paradise Lost*, which she had read by the age of thirteen, and used lines from it for the epigraph for own creation story, *Frankenstein*. These words foreshadow that *Frankenstein*, like every other creation myth that comes to mind, including both the Book of Genesis and *The Epic of Gilgamesh*, conceives of creation as a mixed blessing. They draw a fine line between creation and destruction:

> Did I request thee, Maker, from my clay
> To mould me man? Did I solicit thee
> From darkness to promote me?

Paradise Lost was written, as the poem itself claims, 'to justify the ways of God to men'. Mary Godwin, about to become Mary Shelley, was to discover that it was harder to justify the ways of men to women. Percy Bysshe Shelley, her husband, was a manipulative self-mythologiser. He was conceited, insensitive, and he preferred the company of men who could flatter his monstrous ego to that of his wife who, in the course of their relationship, was to lose four of the five children they conceived together, two from fever within a matter of months. His response to her grief was usually distant.

Frankenstein is alive to the romance of science, a romance that often turns sour. It refers to polar exploration and the use of electricity to engender life as Dr Frankenstein, the creator, prepares to 'infuse a spark of being into the lifeless thing that lay at my feet'. These are ideas that Mary absorbed from the stellar intellectual company kept by her father, the celebrated author of *An Enquiry Concerning Political Justice* (1793). There is a great story of little Mary hiding behind the couch in her father's house while Coleridge, a compulsive talker, recited *The Rime of the Ancient Mariner*. She pays tribute to that poem in *Frankenstein* and, indeed, explores its themes.

But no amount of intellectual ferment or excitement can disguise the fact that Mary's childhood was desperately lonely and that *Frankenstein*—despite the inclination of movie-makers and others to turn the novel into schlock horror—is, at its core, a brilliant study of one of the most mundane and pervasive human experiences, namely loneliness. Her mother, Mary Wollstonecraft, the groundbreaking author of both *A Vindication of the Rights of Men* (1790) and its better-known sequel, *A Vindication of the Rights of Woman* (1792), died ten days after Mary's birth from puerperal fever, a common catastrophe that could have been avoided if the doctor attending the birth had washed his hands. The same thing happened to Mrs Beeton (see Chapter 27), who urged cooks to wash their hands. It's a pity the medical fraternity did not apply her principles of modest practicality.

It is said that Wollstonecraft's infant daughter learnt to read by tracing her fingers through the letters on her mother's tombstone. This could have been a scene from *Frankenstein*. Being the daughter of a famous but absent mother was a burden for Mary: she felt the weight of her expectations but never her love.

William Godwin and Mary Wollstonecraft were at odds with their time in many ways, not least in their unconventional approaches to marriage; Wollstonecraft had children from an earlier relationship. It was hardly surprising that Mary was to follow suit, despite her father's misgivings. Not long after Wollstonecraft's death, Godwin married his excruciating neighbour Mary Jane Clairmont, who brought with her two children who were called, in the supercilious parlance of the time, illegitimate.

Mary could not stand her new stepmother. Shelley, who had been paying court to her father, a publisher, became her parachute. In July 1814, when Mary was still sixteen, they headed off together for Europe. They were joined by Mary's new stepsister, Jane, who later changed her name to Claire. Shelley was having a relationship with both young women. Claire also started a relationship with the leading bad boy of the age, Lord Byron. She had a child to one or other of the men.

Although Mary did profess a belief in open marriage and had liaisons throughout her life with both men and women, you do have to wonder where she found herself in this tangled network. Over many years, she often seems lost, trying to find connections with people that would sustain her. Shelley, who came from aristocratic stock (which he played either up or down, as circumstances required), was providing financial support to the impecunious William Godwin. So Mary needed Shelley to be good to her father even as her father was disowning her. Like countless others in history, Mary Shelley's attempt to escape led to a harsher form of imprisonment. At the time they headed off to Europe, Shelley left behind a pregnant wife, Harriet.

The genesis, to use the word advisedly, of *Frankenstein* is well known. In the gloomy summer on 1816, stuck in Villa Diodati, Byron's holiday house near Geneva, Mary found herself in a party that had been afflicted by what was, for them, a moral crisis. They were bored. So the four—Mary, Shelley, Byron and Byron's doctor, John Polidori—decided to amuse themselves by writing ghost stories. Monopoly and Trivial Pursuit had not yet been invented. Thomas Merton (see Chapter 16) was likewise once in a group that decided to kill a weekend by pumping out a novel. The tiresome vacuity of the exercise brought him one step closer to his commitment to a life of silence.

Mary's life was similarly about to head into deeper waters. She was the only person in the group who took the game seriously. *Frankenstein* is an arresting account of the currents in her life that were leading a naturally creative person into destructive patterns. As she kept working on the book, Shelley read *Paradise Lost* to her as well as *Don Quixote* (see Chapter 33).

Later that year, Mary's half-sister Franny (her mother's daughter) committed suicide. So did Shelley's wife, Harriet, pregnant again to a 'Mr Smith'. This allowed Mary and Shelley to tie the knot, an event she records in her diary with the spare words 'a wedding took place'. The callousness of the couple towards Harriet is staggering but it is clear that Mary was already being tossed about by the storms of anxiety and depression which she would have to weather for much of her life. There are many times in the years ahead—such as in her determination to send her one surviving child, the uninspiring Percy, to school at Harrow—when her strength in the face of adversity is awesome. Her wedding at least brought about a reconciliation with her father.

Frankenstein, published in an edition of five hundred copies on 1 January 1818, has many interests. Nevertheless, it spends more time exploring the nature of language than the scientific process of creating life. The creation scene is a feast of language but light on anything that might pass for scientific specifics. Creation myths throughout history often surf on the need to harness the oceanic movements of language and this is no exception. One of the most touching sequences is the being's own account of his attempt to become part of a human community by learning to speak, then read and write. He longs for connection. He is an improbably fast learner. One of the first books he reads is *Paradise Lost*, where he finds a fellowship with Adam, the creature fashioned from the earth in Chapter 3 of Genesis. The name of Adam actually derives from the Hebrew word for 'earth': he should really be known as Earthling.

> He had come forth from the hands of God a perfect creature, happy and prosperous, guarded by the especial care of his Creator; he allowed to converse with and acquire knowledge from beings of a superior nature: but I was wretched, helpless, and alone.

A good deal of the rest of the story concerns the attempts of the being to find love and to force Frankenstein to make a partner for him. He even says that if Frankenstein agrees, he would happily head off to 'the vast wilds of South America' and keep out of everyone's way.

The being becomes infected with jealousy and curses Frankenstein: 'I will be with you on your wedding night.' But Frankenstein will not co-operate. Again, the novel shares with many creation myths the understanding that the worst thing for a creature to become is something like God. Dr Frankenstein feels he has transgressed the boundaries of his own creature-hood. The power he has found, and which the monster rightly identifies, is terrible. The story will not end well.

~

My search for St Mildred's was fruitless. I was surprised that a Wren church had vanished; it was also the place in which Arthur Phillip, the first governor of New South Wales, had been christened. Surely it was worth preserving. I didn't know that it had been destroyed in an air raid during World War II. Bread Street is now a cavern of soulless offices. On a cold Sunday afternoon, it reminded me of the arctic wastes in which the being is swallowed.

Percy Bysshe Shelley died in a boating accident in 1822. His remains were cremated on the beach but his heart survived. Mary fought with one of Shelley's blokey mates, Leigh Hunt, for the right to possess the relic. She returned from the continent to find that various theatrical versions of *Frankenstein* were making a splash in England. There was no copyright law to protect her from this and she didn't make a penny from the celebrity of the story. For more than thirty years, her life was one of endless financial struggle. Shelley's father was unhelpful. Many people insisted that such a fine novel as *Frankenstein* must have been written by her husband, an impression reinforced by Shelley's ambiguous preface to the first edition.

A revised edition of 1831 attempted to win Mary a place of more conventional respectability. She was a victim of gossip and prejudice, and her unusual lifestyle, especially regarding her sexuality, meant she was ostracised from polite society. She had few friends and even some of those betrayed her. She did it tough. I love her character and her sensuality, even the shock of bright-red hair that she wasn't going to cut to social expectations. When she died, in 1857, the remains of Shelley's dry heart were found in her desk. The being lives on.

CHAPTER 31

Looks

Jane Austen, *Persuasion* (1818)

We shouldn't think that we know all about Jane Austen (1775–1817) just because we've seen a few movies with period costumes. The English countryside of the turn of the nineteenth century was certainly the time and place in which Austen spent her relatively short life. She was the unmarried daughter of a clergyman who gave at least as much time to the flock in his fields as the flock in his church. Fifty years after her death, a nephew, also a clergyman, committed his fading memories of Aunt Jane to paper. He wrote, 'Of events her life was singularly barren: few changes and no great crisis ever broke the smooth current of its course.'

'Barren' is an unfortunate way to describe a childless woman. Few of Austen's contemporaries had the two-hundredth anniversary of their death marked with such warmth and affection, even love, as Austen did in July 2017. She is the many-times-great-grandmother of *Bridget Jones's Diary*, *The Jane Austen Book Club*, *Bride and Prejudice*, *Pride and Prejudice and Zombies* and countless other acts of filial devotion. Austen's life was nothing if not fertile. It wasn't ostentatious. Indeed, the opposite of that word could well be 'austentatious': the fine art of deflecting light from oneself in order to illuminate the follies and pretentions of others. Austen, the writer, had an ambiguous relationship with the other members of her species. Great writers tend to share this.

~

Jane Austen can find the romantic side of even the most unromantic person. This is how I made her acquaintance. I was taught English for the last two years of my schooling by Mr Deegan, a man whose life was spent buffing the patina on antique passions and beliefs. He was eccentric and completely immune to such poisonous pragmatisms as 'Will this be on the exam?' and 'How will this help us in later life?' His refusal to dance to tinny tunes was, in fact, the best thing he could have done for us about later life. Mr Deegan was a card-carrying member of the Bona Mors Society, an organisation whose members prayed for a good death. That was what later life meant to him, I suppose. Some of his students argued at lunchtime about what a good death might mean. If his Bona Mors membership achieved nothing else, it enriched the conversation of adolescent kids. That is a sign of a great teacher.

I saw Mr Deegan five days a week and he always wore the same dark-green suit with a fine lace of dandruff on the collar and shoulders. There was no knowing if the suit had begun life that colour or if it had started out copper and slowly oxidised over the years. The weather made no difference to his appearance. Nor did the occasion, as he wore the same suit and tie to sports day. Perhaps he slept in this outfit: Mr Deegan was what used to be known as a confirmed bachelor and nobody really believed there was any such thing as his personal life. He was frugal, ascetic and—I see now—probably quite anxious. His forehead was furrowed from all the ideas that had been planted there. Little did we know that he had been part of the hockey squad for the Melbourne Olympics until a fractured leg had forced him out. Later, he completed in Rome a doctorate in philosophy.

Now he was consigned to the classroom, where he sat on the desk, put his feet on a chair and railed against any student who failed to sit correctly, especially those putting feet on chairs. Those who interrupted were invariably assigned an essay on the topic 'Silence is golden', a penalty that was so frequently applied that there developed a covert market in suitable one-page writings. They would make an excellent anthology if they could be retrieved but Mr Deegan was famous for not reading essays. Legend had it that one boy submitted his mother's lasagne recipe as an essay on *Hamlet* and received an A. It must have been a good recipe.

His lunch was a handful of nuts that he counted on the desk in front of us, a bit like Scrooge counting his coins. My friend Matthew said that people who count nuts must themselves be nuts. Yet Mr Deegan loved the bawdiness of Shakespeare and explained it with a kind of life-affirming heartiness that has been completely blanched by the sexual correctness of today.

Jane Austen made Mr Deegan laugh. His laughter made us laugh. It rattled every bone in his fragile body as well as his teeth. When we studied *Emma* (1815), he paused at a particular description of Mr Elton, another clergyman and one of the central figures in Austen's exquisite satire of self-importance. Mr Elton has the temerity to be in love with the wrong person. At one point, at the height of his romantic ambitions, he is described as 'spruce, black and smiling'. What might the word 'black' mean in this context? It nails Elton's sartorial fussiness with a single word and makes 'smiling' seem nothing but fake. We were hardly mature students of literature and had been used to laughing at every appearance of the word 'intercourse', a frequent visitor to Austen's prose but always fully dressed. The description of Elton as 'spruce, black and smiling' moved us to another level of appreciation.

'It's a miracle of a line, isn't it,' said Mr Deegan. 'What do you think, Petry?'

'I'd say it's a miracle, sir.'

In my last year, I was the only student to enrol in an extra English unit, so I had Mr Deegan all to myself for two classes a week. They were scheduled for 8 a.m. because they couldn't otherwise be accommodated in the timetable. If I was late, which was usually the case, Deegan would already have started, sharing his enthusiasm with an empty room, declaiming the genius of Jane Austen to the back wall.

~

That year, our tiny class studied *Persuasion*, published after Austen's death, the last and in some ways most sturdy of Austen's completed novels, one that has grown on me over the years. It is a work in which a wider world is more palpable. It is a mistake, however, to think that broader concerns were absent from Austen's life. Her first birthday in 1776 coincided with a requirement that her father hold a special church service to pray that the American rebels would be defeated. Those prayers do not seem to have influenced the Almighty, or perhaps they did but not to oblige the English. You can never tell what prayers achieve.

Jane's older brother, George, lived with significant intellectual disabilities and was unable to develop language skills. Jane, ten years younger, was able to communicate with him in sign language. It is curious that people with such disabilities are seldom if ever visible in her fiction.

A broader concern that does knock on the door of her fiction is the slave trade, as it does in the work of the Brontës (see Chapter 29), often disguised under the banner of economic interests in the Caribbean—an important aspect of the fortunes, for example, of both Sir Thomas Bertram in *Mansfield Park* (1814) and Mrs Smith in *Persuasion*. The slave trade is explicitly used as an image in *Emma*, where Jane Fairfax compares it with the business of hiring governesses and Mrs Elton declares herself an abolitionist. When Mr Elton is described as 'spruce, black and smiling', the word 'black' is also a byword for servitude, even slavery.

Persuasion is set in the wake of the Napoleonic Wars and these make their presence felt in the story. Up until now, most of the characters in Austen have had a passive relationship with money. They either have it, inherit it or marry it. Or not. But in all events they are enslaved to it, a fact which

Austen documents to the last shilling. In *Persuasion*, one of the central characters, Captain Wentworth, actually makes money. Moreover, he profits from war:

> He had not made less than twenty thousand pounds by the war. Here was a fortune at once; besides which, there would be the chance of what might be done in any future war.

The plot also includes women who are familiar with warships:

> 'I do assure you, ma'am,' pursued Mrs Croft, 'that nothing can exceed the accommodations of a man of war… When you come to a frigate, of course, you are more confined.'

Persuasion follows a love story that does not move in a simple linear direction. Eight years before the novel opens, Anne Elliot had followed the advice of others and rejected the hand of Captain Wentworth. She now regrets this. A turn of events brings Wentworth back into her circle and, little by little, the couple negotiate various obstacles and get back together. Austen is alive to the power of sexual attraction. People sometimes think otherwise, but Austen is subtle rather than coy, suggestive rather than prim.

There is one scene in *Persuasion* that makes this point beautifully. On a visit from the countryside to Lyme Regis, Anne is part of a group that happens to come across Mr Elliot, the cousin to whom her family estate is entailed. It might help the family situation if he and Anne were to marry. Anyway, before Mr Elliot's identity is revealed, a fuse is lit:

When they came to the steps, leading upwards from the beach, a gentleman at the same moment preparing to come down, politely drew back, and stopped to give them way. They ascended and passed him; and as they passed, Anne's face caught his eye, and he looked at her with a degree of earnest admiration, which she could not be insensible of. She was looking remarkably well...It was evident that the gentleman (completely a gentleman in manner) admired her exceedingly. Captain Wentworth looked round at her instantly in a way which shewed his noticing of it. He gave her a momentary glance—a glance of brightness.

Just follow the eyes in this vignette. Elliott looks at Anne. Wentworth does the same. 'Earnest admiration' and 'admired her exceedingly' are phrases loaded with desire. 'A glance of brightness' is the same, if not more so. The sexuality of this scene is intense. It sets up the rivalry that will control the rest of the novel and makes it clear that this rivalry is in some significant measure about sex. The restraint only adds to the charged nature of the encounter.

We are in danger of creating a world that is bored by sex. Sex is analysed and discussed and measured and judged to the point that it has become like a pair of pyjamas that have been too long in service. It lacks freshness and surprise. There are authorities who want to protect young people from all the nervousness and confusion, tentativeness and insecurity that made the discovery of sex a source of wonder and comedy for countless generations. In this context, it is hardly surprising that Jane Austen remains close to the top of every survey of readers' all-time favourite books. She does more for the imagination that all the policies and procedures under the sun.

CHAPTER 32

This Bed Thy Centre Is

John Donne, 'The Sunne Rising'
(early seventeenth century)

My father died when I was in Year 12, three weeks before I began the final exams. He had been sick for a long time, since I was in Year 6, but in the end his death was unexpected: it took us all by surprise.

I spent quite a lot of time that year in the volatile company of a figure whose effervescent, hard-working and outrageous writing I still turn to in times of need. This was John Donne (1572–1631), maker of the kind of erotic verse that is hardly designed to quieten the spirit of young people. He wrote a poem about a flea in which he says how much he envies the insect because 'it sucks me first, and now sucks thee'.

He also wrote a famous poem that I committed to memory and recited to myself over and over. 'The Sunne Rising' imagines the sun looking through the window at early morning lovers. It is about finding the entire world in a shared bed. I had no prospect at that stage of experiencing anything like this in reality. The poem did more for my imagination than it could do for itself.

John Donne can be a bewildering figure. He became an Anglican priest in 1615 basically because he was desperate for a job. He was pragmatic about many things in his life, and religion was one of them. There are times when everybody has to take a job just for the money, but it's not everybody who takes one of those jobs and then produces work that money can't buy.

Donne was a Londoner to the core of his being. His father was an ironmonger who died when Donne was young. Donne decided early that he was never going to make his living in trade. He was going to be a gentleman, and by the age of twelve he was at Oxford University. His love of books and learning was authentic and became a mainstay of his life. The reason he went to university so young was that, at age sixteen, students were required to swear allegiance to the monarch, Elizabeth I, and Donne wanted to finish his studies before he had to do that.

Donne was a Catholic. He wasn't just any Catholic, either. He was directly descended on his mother's side from the martyr Sir Thomas More. His uncle Jasper became a Jesuit priest, and was imprisoned and tortured in the Tower of London. Donne visited Jasper there as a young man and never forgot the experience. Donne's younger brother, Henry, was put in the Tower for sheltering a Catholic priest and died there in 1593. His mother, Elizabeth, was forced to live in exile on the continent for years because of her Catholic beliefs.

Donne was not prepared to pay the same price for his convictions or even to admire the commitment of those who did. He later put forward the belief that martyrdom is actually a form of suicide: an avoidable death caused by an inability to think straight.

John Donne was certainly ambitious. He published very little of his poetry in his lifetime because he considered publication an ungentlemanly activity. It is likely that he was in the theatre at the same time as Shakespeare, and some scholars have speculated about their possible collaboration, but Shakespeare's audience was much broader. Donne's early poetry, wonderfully ribald and witty, often dealt with sex and romance. It was circulated among his friends and associates. Meanwhile, Donne was working his way up the social ladder. He served abroad in Ireland and Spain before landing an important post as a civil servant. His sharp mind and efficiency made a strong impression. He was going places.

Yet there is always more to anybody's story. Donne's first and in some ways most eloquent biographer, Izaac Walton (who wrote *The Compleat Angler*, 1653: still one of the greatest sporting books ever written), thought that the poet's marriage to Anne More was a big mistake. He called it the 'remarkable error of his life'. This is hardly fair but it was undoubtedly a costly relationship. Ann was ten years younger than her husband and married Donne in a clandestine marriage in 1601. The wedding took place in Advent, which was against church law, and Anne, as a minor, should have had the approval of both her father and her guardian. She had neither. Heaven knows why the couple went about things in a secretive manner but when the marriage came to light, Donne was imprisoned for a brief time, lost his job and spent the next ten years excluded from the company he relished. He was forced to move to the country and live in much reduced circumstances, comforted mostly by his books.

The couple had twelve children, five of whom died young, three of those in the space of a year. One of Donne's many biographers, John Stubbs, writes: 'he found that having a family made him feel lonely rather than connected, because of the great pressure his wife and children put on him…Without a fitting place in the world, he was an unhappy patriarch.' Donne found living amid a brood of children a lonely experience. He was absent for long periods.

For all the pain, Donne loved Anne profoundly. She is the inspiration of some exquisite poetry, much of it reflecting the ambivalence and struggle of love. He was devastated when she died in 1617, and before long his poetry began to wrestle with the same intensity with God as it had done with love. Donne's religious poetry is among the most searching ever written. It shares the wit and inventiveness of his erotic verse. It testifies to the life-and-death struggle to understand life and death. He may have got into the business to make ends meet, but it is impossible to believe that is the whole story.

~

Donne's work late in his life as dean of St Paul's Cathedral was torn between delicate political ballet on the one hand and coping with his ill health on the other. His last sermon, 'Death's Duell', is famous. It was preached while he hardly had enough breath left in him to speak and the effect is histrionic. But a few years earlier, in 1623, he was ravaged by disease, probably typhoid, and thought his hour had come. He published *Devotions Upon Emergent Occasions*, spiritual prose alive to all the possibilities of language and imagery. Parts of it, including Meditation XVII, are often quoted. It touches upon the longing to belong which is close to the heart of Donne's soul: 'No man is an island, entire of itself.' Other parts deserve to be better known:

> All mankind is of one Author and is one volume; when one man dies, one Chapter is not torn out of the book, but translated into a better language; and every Chapter must be so translated; God employs several translators: some pieces are translated by age, some by sickness, some by war, some by justice; but God's hand is in every translation; and his hand shall bind up all our scattered leaves again, for that Library where every book shall lie open to one another.

~

Donne's erotic verse rescues sex from the rubble of consumer clichés and gives voice to all the anxiety that comes with getting close to a real person. His religious verse brings erotic intensity to the pursuit of faith.

One of his last works, 'A Hymn to God, My God, in My Sickness', compares his dying body to a map. It has taken him on the voyage of exploration which has been his life and asks where his home is to be found. I read this poem when my father died one grey Sunday morning and it reached past the callous exterior I cultivated in order to cope. The poem turned the humdrum necessities of a bed in the corner of Ward 17 in

Sydney Hospital, where a nurse discreetly drew the curtain after Dad died and wrote something in biro in a plastic folder, into something far more extraordinary and even dramatic. There is no starched white linen in Donne. Every bed in his work, used either for sleeping or waking, for making love or dying, is ruffled:

> Since I am coming to that holy room
> Where, with Thy choir of saints forevermore,
> I shall be made Thy Music; as I come
> I tune the instrument here at the door,
> And what I must do then, think here before.

CHAPTER 33

The Ingenious Gentleman

Miguel de Cervantes, *Don Quixote* (1605)

I only know one joke and I have learnt to make the most of it. It has got me through countless school camps and excursions. So I have no intention of wasting it here.

Shakespeare (see Chapter 2) was great at getting the most out of a joke.

But nobody holds a candle to the work of the hapless and often destitute Miguel de Cervantes Saavedra (1547–1616). *Don Quixote* is a book of almost a thousand pages built around a single joke. The joke is that a middlebrow knight becomes so addicted to novels of romance and chivalry that his brains dry up and he starts to think he is living one of those far-fetched stories. Windmills become giants, peasants become princes, a barber's bowl becomes a helmet. He sets out to travel the world in search of courtly love and, indeed, he does reach the furthest corners of human experience, although he never needs to travel more than about fifty kilometres from where he starts in order to do so. The one gag never stales.

~

Legend has it that *Macbeth* and *Don Quixote* appeared in the same year. It also holds that Cervantes and Shakespeare died on the same day in 1616. Certainly they died in the same week, which would have made for interesting traffic at the pearly gates. I imagine that Cervantes would have chided Shakespeare for writing about so many wars when he, Cervantes, had actually fought in them, notably the Battle of Lepanto where he lost the use of his left arm. Had it been his right arm, he might never have composed his enormous masterpiece and we would all be much poorer. Shakespeare wrote about jails of every kind; Cervantes spent five years in one in Algiers where he was sold as a slave, making some valiant attempts to escape before his family raised the ransom.

Shakespeare, on the other hand, might have ribbed Cervantes for undermining his business model: the stage and public performance. The enormous popularity of *Don Quixote* had a role in creating one of the cornerstones of our culture, the figure sitting on his or her own, reading for entertainment. King Philip III of Spain once commented that if he saw a person laughing alone, they were either mad or reading *Don Quixote*. Don Quixote himself was both these things: a mad reader.

Of course, Cervantes and Shakespeare never met. If they had, Shakespeare would have been more likely to write a play about the improbable figure of Cervantes than the other way around. Shakespeare tried to make money by making sense of the world, for which endeavours he is rightly applauded. Cervantes was able to make neither money nor much sense of the world, which is why the work for which he is celebrated, *The Ingenious Gentleman Don Quixote of La Mancha*, makes such bizarre good sense. It is a book which taught the world a new way to laugh: not a bad strategy for dealing with the craziness of life.

Perhaps that is the reason it remains one of the most popular books ever pirated, a form of theft that can take place in many ways. Don Quixote's horse, a poor old bag of bones, was called Rocinante. In *Travels with Charley* (1962), John Steinbeck calls his motorhome Rocinante. In Graham Greene's *Monsignor Quixote* (1982), the priest's car is called Rocinante. My brother Joe called his first car, a hapless VW that made more sound than movement, Rocinante. A lot of people have had a Rocinante in the garage at some stage.

~

I owe my relationship with *Don Quixote* to a friendship with Peter Steele. It's a shame that not more people have heard of Peter. He is one of those figures whose CV does nothing to capture his spirit nor his breadth—like Wallace Stevens working in his insurance firm, or William Carlos Williams making house visits as a doctor in New Jersey to help bring hundreds of babies into the world, or John Donne's endless quest to make ends meet (see Chapter 32).

Peter was not a career person. He was a priest and a poet. Born in Perth in 1939, he joined the Jesuits aged seventeen and spent the next six years in an isolated castle at Watsonia in

Melbourne that was later sold to the Department of Corrections as fit for their purposes. From the mid-1960s his working life was centred mostly in the English Department at the University of Melbourne, where he eventually gained a personal chair. He died in 2012 after struggling with liver cancer which, he was pleased to discover, owed nothing to drink. Peter Steele was also one of the major religious poets of the twentieth century. He was a significant inspiration to Seamus Heaney and Peter Porter. His poetry was earthy, elusive, recherché, comic, erudite, sometimes difficult and often tender.

I knew Peter Steele for about thirty years and could share many stories about him. A good number of these stories have a delightful flavour of implausibility. Peter was a true original, one of the few I have met. There wasn't a cliché in him. Yet, for most of the time we were friends, he presented as a stocky middle-aged academic and priest. The package was unprepossessing. He was alive to the play of imagery against substance everywhere in the world but he did little to cultivate his own image. His sunglasses were so old that they had come back into fashion. The same was true of his trench coat.

Inside a plain exterior was a universe of wonders. Peter's conversation was an endless series of brilliant postcards from all the places that his mind had visited. Peter loved light. This is curious because he was a dreadful insomniac. The kind of word he loved was 'lucent', an expression that tugs at the imagination precisely because it is a little strange, not the sort of word you hear at the supermarket checkout when you're buying lightbulbs. Yet what it describes, the glow caused by light, is very familiar. Part of Peter's gift was to restore the oddness of things to which familiarity can breed indifference.

His first collection of poetry was called *Word from Lilliput* (1973). Peter had a life-long relationship with Jonathan Swift, a figure he resembled in ways other than wardrobe. Peter wrote his doctorate on Swift, later published as a book subtitled *Preacher and Jester* (1972), an apt description for Peter himself. He loved the eighteenth century. For him, it was the best time in which to laugh. Swift and Sterne tickled him into deep thought; they are writers for whom the absurd is the door to a fund of common sense. He believed that Fielding was the closest English literature ever got to Cervantes.

For Peter, there was an important spirituality in satire because satire refuses to take the human ego too seriously. This was central to his love of *Don Quixote*. Peter described himself as a celebrant of life, which meant that he understood humans are essentially laughable. He shared this insight with G. K. Chesterton (see Chapter 21), who was an important early influence on him. You can hear the echoes of Chesterton's merry paradoxes in some of Peter's prose.

Over the years, Peter battled with lowness of spirit and depression. Sometimes he had to work hard to find the sense of hope that supports his work. That is why he understood the message of the light that has come into our darkness, the lightness into our heaviness. He understood death and grief, and the intimacies they create over distances that can be impossible to bridge in life. Here is a poem he wrote on the death of his younger brother:

No day goes by without your haunting me,
You, whose tongue was always heavy with silence.

Watching myself taped, a mouth pouring
Word on crested word, I am ashamed

To have outlived you, whom I first saw huddled
Behind glass some wars and loves ago.

There is, as your brooding gaze always implied,
Nothing to say. But as I back towards

Your veiled country, let me say only
That you were never slight, nor I the rock.

~

I lived in the same Jesuit Community, Campion College, as Peter Steele for five years in the early 1980s. It was a remarkable place, not least because it housed so many eccentric gentlemen. The Jesuits had acquired a grand old mansion, built by the Gibson of Foy & Gibson fame, a merchant who had wanted a residence high on Studley Park Hill where he could look over the world of his workers on the industrial flats of Abbotsford and Collingwood below.

The order added a cheap brick-veneer extension in which lived we students on the ground floor and a riot of retired Jesuits on the upper floor. Only three people actually lived in the uncomfortable bedrooms under the great dome of the mansion at the front that looked impressive but lacked any creature comforts. Peter Steele was one of them. The others, Charlie and Robin, were both intellectually disabled.

Robin had grown up in Kew Cottages from the age of about three and later became famous as the 'dancing man of

Kew'. You can google that phrase to enter a little of his world. Robin laughed halfway through jokes because he never understood a punchline, only that people were enjoying themselves. He seldom forgot a name; Peter, on the other hand, often struggled for names and his greetings sometimes resorted to the unpoetic 'mate'. Once, Robin was distraught that his girlfriend might be pregnant because they'd been on a picnic and both dozed off on the same rug. He thought this is what people meant by sleeping together.

Charlie and Robin were beautiful people, and Peter was very much at home in their company. He was especially close to Robin and would have enjoyed the irony of their both dying in the same week, in 2012. They were not quite Sancho and Quixote but they were yin and yang. Peter was humble in unnerving ways. He was also a torrential writer, referring to himself as 'a broken hydrant'. Many nights, you would see Peter retiring to his room with a washing basket full of books and his laundry in a battered old briefcase. He read through the night, feeding voraciously on the written word. He had that in common with his muse, Don Quixote. The difference was that Peter, unlike most people, could not easily deceive himself. Peter's openness to life's possibilities helped me to leave the mansion and go to live in a community of homeless people in the inner city called The Way (see Chapter 17). In *Expatriates* (1985), Peter said that he believed in 'the quixotification of Sancho and the sanchification of Quixote'. This means, I think, that the servant needs to dream and the adventurer needs to serve. It means that some of us need to get off our horses and others need to get on them.

~

Don Quixote promised his faithful companion, Sancho Panza, the throne of an island kingdom. Sancho is a better friend than Don Quixote deserves. In the novel, some of the people who prey on the knight errant decide to play a hoax on poor Sancho and carry him off, with mock solemnity, to a village which they convince him is an island and he its lord. Surprisingly, Sancho turns out to be quite a good ruler. His subjects present him with a number of riddles to which he responds with common sense, developed in part from his love of proverbs and aphorisms, many of which he confuses and misquotes.

Just because Sancho speaks the language of greeting cards, it doesn't mean what he says is silly. His relationship with Don Quixote is profound: a lover can often accept and cherish parts of their beloved which the beloved has built elaborate fantasies to disguise. One sad thing about the Knight of Doleful Countenance, as the don is known, is that he fantasises about the ladies for whom he will undertake deeds of chivalry. Yet they don't exist. All the time, Sancho is by his side. The reality is more beautiful than the fantasy, only less glamorous. The real is more ideal than the ideal. Don Quixote can't see this: his imagination has been straitjacketed by the popular culture of his time, namely junk novels about knights and chivalry, the contemporary equivalent of reality TV. For him, madness is alienation from reality.

One of the riddles Sancho has to solve in his kingdom concerns a bridge across a river. On one side of the bridge were a courthouse and a gallows. In the courthouse, there were four judges, positioned to administer an unusual law which required anyone who passed over the bridge to state their destination and their reason for going there. Those who answered truthfully were allowed to pass unhindered. Those who lied were put to death on the gallows.

Once, though, a certain traveller announced under oath that he was crossing the bridge because he was going to die on the gallows which he could see on the other side. This created a quandary. If the man was telling the truth and intended to die on the gallows, then he was, by that very fact, required to go free. But if he was lying and was not going to die on the gallows then, obviously, he should die on the gallows. If he was hanged, he would have been truthful and justice would have been defeated. If he was allowed to go free, he was lying and justice would again have been defeated. How was justice to be served?

The courtiers tell Sancho they have approached him because of his incisive mind. He corrects them, tells them he is a blockhead, then says that the obvious thing to do is to let the man go free. The reason is that it is always better to do good than to do evil and that in cases of doubt, leniency and mercy are to be preferred. It is a disarming answer. He defeats the riddle by reminding his listeners that life is not an intellectual exercise; justice is not an abstract notion. If you can find the person inside the riddle, it isn't a game anymore.

CHAPTER 34

By Spells and Medicines

William Shakespeare, *Othello* (c. 1603)

I have a *Works of Shakespeare* that I picked up at a jumble sale for $4.50. It has a padded cover and gilt-edged pages, making it feel more like an object for a shelf rather than a book to feast upon. The tiny typeface suggests it is not a volume that you could read comfortably. Yet this *Works* is a chest of drawers with little things hidden inside. There is a presentation plate that indicates the book was awarded to Miss M. O'Loughlin as Dux of the School at the Convent Notre Dame de Sion High School in Bairnsdale in Victoria at Christmas in an unspecified year, I'd say in the 1920s. The plate also acknowledges Miss M. O'Loughlin's success in English, French, Geography, Music, Physiology and Maths. There was a moment, back in time, when this impressive volume was the centrepiece of the final gathering of a regional school community.

There are two bookmarks inside which tell a different, more private, story. They are both made by hand from scraps of ribbon and cardboard. The first says: 'Happy Christmas to my darling little Molly from her old mother. Sion. Xmas 1920.' I suspect the 'old mother' was a nun who clearly loved teaching Molly, the prize student. It was lodged in the final scene of *Othello*. The second says: 'Hail Glorious St Patrick Sale 1920', and had found its way into the pages of *The Tempest* (see Chapter 2). The book acknowledges the achievement of a bright young woman who, in the years immediately following the destruction of war, was a source of hope and pride. Perhaps she found her way to university. Who knows? But the book is also a shrine to a relationship between a teacher and a student, and those bookmarks meant enough to Molly that she moved them into the prize, turning it from a trophy into a small tribute to her teacher.

I love teaching Shakespeare and tell my students, perhaps hopefully, that they should have read the entire *Complete Works* by the time they are twenty-five. One time, a boy called Pat responded gleefully: 'Challenge accepted.' If every teenager were like that, you'd pay money to take the class. But they aren't. So I tell them that if they are only going to read one play, then make it *Othello*.

~

I encountered *Othello* when I was at school, which must have been soon after it was first performed. In those days—actually less than a decade after the assassination of Martin Luther King— our attention was drawn to the manner in which Shakespeare handles issues of race. These are live wires, even now.

Othello, a military general and a Moor, is black. He falls in love with and marries a young white Venetian woman called Desdemona. This is such a scandal that the marriage takes place in secret: the city of Venice accepts Othello because he is useful and has 'done the state some service'. They want his military prowess but they don't want him, at least not as a family member. Iago, Othello's third-in-command, sets out to slowly and inexorably destroy the relationship between Othello and Desdemona.

I have never taught a student who was not fascinated by the subtlety and skill Iago brings to the art of destruction. William Booth, the founder of the Salvation Army, bemoaned the fact that the devil had all the best tunes. Iago certainly leads the band in *Othello*; he even uses the image of music to describe the way he plays Othello. He manipulates everyone, except possibly his wife, Emilia, who knows what he's like.

In the first scene, Iago, along with a poor fool called Roderigo whom Iago uses as both a toy and a moneybox, stands beneath the window of Brabantio, Desdemona's father, and, under cover of dark, tells Brabantio that his daughter is being screwed by a black man: 'You'll have your daughter covered with a Barbary horse.' Barbary horses came from Africa. There is a connection between being an animal and black. Even more explicitly, Iago yells:

> Even now, now, very now, an old black ram
> Is tupping your white ewe.

The emphasis on 'now, now, very now' creates an immediate visual picture for the distressed father. Iago, apart from all else, is a pornographer. His approach to sexuality is entirely visual: he is a spectator who reduces others to the same level of looking through windows. In the middle of the play, after Iago has said 'look to your wife' and has begun to insinuate his poison into Othello's mind, Othello demands visual evidence of Desdemona's infidelity: 'Give me the ocular proof.' Iago creates a pornographic scene to dissuade Othello:

> Would you, the supervisor, grossly gape on,
> Behold her topped?

Confronted with this image, Othello will tragically settle for 'imputation and strong circumstances'.

The theme of race infiltrates the whole play. No matter what he does, Othello will always be the lover with a 'sooty bosom'.

But these days, we are more likely to bring another concern to an encounter with *Othello*. Othello is from an Islamic background and this too is used to demonise him. In the dying minutes of the play, when the full extent of a needless catastrophe has come to light, Othello stabs himself. As he does so, he imagines he is 'a malignant and turbaned Turk' whom he had once met in Aleppo, a city whose present tragedy bites the conscience of the world. Othello does not kill a Venetian general. He kills an upstart Muslim.

The Moor encounters a level of religious prejudice that would satisfy even the most rabid political commentator these days. At the very moment Iago is salivating over the 'old black ram…tupping your white ewe', he tells Brabantio: 'the devil will make a grandsire of you.' In other words, Othello is from the murkiest corner of the religious world, part of Satan's tribe. Trying to explain how his daughter could have fallen for 'such a thing as thou', Brabantio insists that 'thou has enchanted her' and put her 'in chains of magic'. The handkerchief that Desdemona mislays and which Iago then exploits to carry out his plans was first given to Othello's mother by an Egyptian 'charmer' who put 'magic in the web of it'. There is a haze of sorcery and witchcraft drawn over Othello's spiritual upbringing. His wife, by way of contrast, is 'divine Desdemona'.

The truth is both more simple and more complex. Shakespeare was fascinated by disguise and deception. He would hardly have been in the theatre business otherwise, and for him it was, indeed, first and foremost a business. It is astonishing that he created *Othello* two or three years after *Hamlet*, two or three years before *Macbeth* and *King Lear*. In the first decade of the seventeenth century Shakespeare was, to use a phrase my students prefer, on fire. He took the English language to places it had never been before. He said things about the human condition that had never been said in the same way. Yet for him it was a job. The name of the Globe Theatre suggested that, perched on the bank of the Thames, it could contain the entire world. But it was also a workplace where people had to be paid.

Iago is a master of deception. 'I am not what I am,' he tells Roderigo, and he means it.

Not I for love or duty,
But seeming so, for my peculiar end.

He pretends to be loyal to Othello; to support Michael Cassio, Othello's second-in-command; and to counsel Desdemona. Nobody sees through him until it is too late. Othello is up against an irresistible force. But he is not entirely blameless. Early in the play, he talks about his upbringing. From the age of seven, he was a soldier. He has gone to all parts of the world, including the mystical lands of cannibals and the Anthropophagi described by Herodotus (see Chapter 37). Desdemona used to listen to these stories as he shared them with her father and fell in love with him:

> She loved me for the dangers I had passed,
> And I loved her that she did pity them.
> This only is the witchcraft I have used.

Take those words in slow motion. Othello has not experienced much tenderness, so his response to Desdemona is understandable. But it is all about him. She loves him for his courage. He loves her because she loves him. What was ever in the relationship for Desdemona?

The word 'honest' is a character in the play. It is used on scores of occasions, each time with a slightly different shade of meaning. The manner in which this one word gains so many subtle flavours is a tour de force. It is also a clue to the slippery nature of evil. People have tried to identify Iago's motives. He was passed over for promotion. He has a chip on his shoulder about being not as well bred as the guy who got the job, Cassio. He wants money. He thinks it's possible Othello has slept with his wife. He could even have a crush on Othello and want to destroy his marriage. Perhaps he simply enjoys making trouble.

Many other possible motives have been suggested as well. But the poet Coleridge, never at a loss for a word, described all this as 'the motive-hunting of a motiveless malignity'. It is a scandal that Iago survives at the end of the play. He vows that he will never say another word, and he doesn't. He is taken away, silent and in chains:

> Demand me nothing: what you know, you know:
> From this time forth I never will speak word.

This is a powerful truth. Evil continues to walk the earth. It is often unexplained.

~

I have a special copy of *Othello* that was given to me at the end of his schooling by a fine young man whose father had died during that year. The illness had been sudden and devastating. Laurence, an only child, had a lot to think about, and he did that thinking with grace and honesty. He wrote inside the book: 'Your guidance in my first year of literature helped me fall in love with the subject. Thank you for the friendly chats we often shared.'

I was touched by those words and the generosity towards others that they carried. It may be that *Othello* helped Laurence in that year. I like to think so. It is a work about the high price of love. It speaks across four hundred years.

CHAPTER 35

Plenty

Geoffrey Chaucer, *The Canterbury Tales* (c. 1390)

There was every reason for Geoffrey Chaucer (1342–1400) to have become a tedious bore. First of all, his father was a wine merchant, a position that was then described as 'vintner'. If the wine trade of fourteenth century London bore any resemblance to the current wine trade, this meant that Chaucer grew up in a world of inconsequential small talk and high-sounding verbiage.

Chaucer became a diplomat, and if diplomacy of that time was similar to the current equivalent, this meant that he made a living out of inconsequential small talk and high-sounding verbiage. He married advisedly rather than passionately. He and Philippa had three children, a neat family. They lived mostly apart and, when she died in 1387, he promised that he would not again 'falle of weddynge in the trappe'. He was a reliable but dreary public servant for whom writing was a sideline: for years he was in charge of collecting 'petty custom' on imported wool.

Chaucer was lucky to escape the bubonic plague that swept the metropolis in the decade of his birth, a catastrophe that may have done for a third of London's population, and nothing makes for more boring small talk than medical near misses. Chaucer was an expert on luck of every kind. As his fortunes rose and fell with the political tide, he was imprisoned in a dark cell at one stage and provided with a residence over Aldgate at another, one of the best views in London for anyone who liked watching people, as Chaucer surely did. G. K. Chesterton (see Chapter 21) said that Chaucer was 'a lucky and lonely elf, who found a sunbeam and danced in it'.

Late in life, around 1389, he became clerk of the king's works, which meant that he was ultimately responsible for making sure the plumbing worked in a long list of royal residences. No doubt there was plenty of ordure to contend with in the position, but none of it would have made for interesting conversation. He also looked after repairs but rivets are hardly riveting.

Yet Chaucer is anything but boring. He is as much fun as anyone who ever wrote in what we now call the English language, partly because he was one of the first to discover how much merriment you can get out of English. He was probably born in the same year as Julian of Norwich, the first woman to write a book in English, *Revelations of Divine Love* (c. 1395). Julian's solitary life as an anchorite, possibly a device for coping with plague or living in its aftermath, was the polar opposite of Chaucer's famous celebration of people on the move to Canterbury in springtime. Julian also took pleasure in the springtime of her language. She wrote: 'all shall be well, and all manner of thing shall be well', which was, as a nun once told me, all well and good for her. Julian loved teasing out delicate images. She wrote that our soul is enclosed in our bodies 'as in a beautiful purse'. Chaucer, on the other hand, was like a kid with a new toy, figuring out how many games he could play with this unbreakable new language.

The seventeenth-century poet John Dryden, himself a bit of a bore who took a chainsaw to the great forest of Shakespeare in order to tidy it up, said of *The Canterbury Tales*, Chaucer's masterpiece, 'Here is God's plenty.' He was right. *The Canterbury Tales* is teeming with life, both sacred and profane. For Chaucer, that was a false dichotomy, as it should be for everyone.

Despite my facetious remarks, Chaucer in fact met a lot of people and travelled widely, both at home and abroad. He also was extremely well read and loved *The Consolation of Philosophy* (c. 524 CE) by the Roman author Boethius. So when he came to assemble the cast of twenty-nine storytellers, each of whom is on a pilgrimage to the shrine of St Thomas à Becket in Canterbury Cathedral, he drew from every rank and position in society. Chaucer was familiar with medieval mystery plays that exploited stock figures such as Adam, Eve and Lucifer. To us, these works now seem static. *The Canterbury Tales* is also replete with familiar types: a knight, a pardoner, a cleric, a nun, a cook and so on. But each of them is individually created because each has an individual story to tell.

Chaucer is one of the first writers for whom we can compile a biography: we know quite a lot about him. This marks the beginning of modern literature, where works are ascribed to individuals rather than developed by communities. He began parts of *The Canterbury Tales* in his middle years, including the lengthy 'The Knight's Tale', a seemly and elegant exposition of the nature of courtly love. 'The Knight's Tale' is beautiful. But the real fun starts after Chaucer had retired from public service, or been forced to retire as his patrons lost influence, and could suit himself. This is when he wrote most of the collection which appears to have been incomplete when Chaucer's career was interrupted by death; it is also vaguely possible that he intended the work to have been left with a kind of 'finish it yourself' feeling.

After a lifetime of minding his Ps and Qs, Chaucer had decided to grow old disgracefully, which is a kind of grace. So he followed the demure 'The Knight's Tale' with a story of joyous ribaldry, 'The Miller's Tale', that provides a healthy reminder that, for most of our history, sex has been a source of comedy and a doorway to the absurd. God knows when it became a topic for furrowed brows. 'The Miller's Tale' is told by an individual that the knight could only have encountered in a circus such as a pilgrimage characterised by 'sundry folk happening then to fall / In fellowship'. It may owe something to the inexhaustible bawdiness of *The Decameron* (c. 1353) by Giovanni Boccaccio. *The Decameron* is a collection of tales told by ten well-to-do young people who are seeking shelter from the plague that hit Florence in 1348. Fearing for their lives, they pass the time joking about sex. The context of

The Canterbury Tales is different. Nobody in it is seeking refuge. The characters and their stories belong to the open road and the shared table. Even as a slightly older man (he never reached old age), Chaucer was still discovering an appetite for the world.

Chaucer's energy as a storyteller is irresistible. 'The Miller's Tale' tells of a young woman (Alison) who is married to a carpenter (a reeve) called John. Two young students, Absalom and Nicholas, want to seduce Alison while John is away for work. Their manoeuvres are worthy of any comedian you care to name. Eventually, Alison sticks her bum through a toilet opening in the dark so Absalom can kiss her cheek. Then Nicholas, who has been taking his pleasure with Alison, thinks he can get Absalom to kiss him on the backside as well. But this time Absalom is waiting with a red-hot poker. Nevill Coghill's modern version ends with the memorable lines:

> And Nicholas is branded on the bum
> And God bring us all to Kingdom Come.

It is no surprise that the reeve wants to tell the next story as an act of revenge against the miller. And so the journey continues.

~

There is at least as much about food in *The Canterbury Tales* as there is about sex. 'The General Prologue'—probably written towards the end of the process, as most introductions, prefaces and overtures tend to be—presents each of the pilgrims one by one. Much of the time, Chaucer introduces a character in terms of their relationship with food and the rituals of eating. So the knight is first presented as one who 'often sat at table in the chair / Of honour' and his son, the Squire, 'carved to serve his father at the table'. The monk's attitude to sacred texts is likened to food and the friar tends to hang around with people who can provide him with fine cuisine. The epicurean tendencies of the Franklin (a person with an estate) are measured in kilojoules:

> His bread, his ale were finest of the fine
> And no one had a better stock of wine.
> His house was never short of bake-meat pies.

This contrasts with the nun, a woman of perfect manners. Chaucer creates her whole character from watching the way she eats:

> At meat her manners were well taught withal;
> No morsel from her lips did she let fall,
> Nor dipped her fingers in the sauce too deep;
> But she could carry a morsel up and keep
> The smallest drop from falling on her breast.

Sharing food is the context for the whole of *The Canterbury Tales*. It begins at an inn called The Tabard in Southwark. At the end, the prize for the best storyteller is to be a meal, paid for by all the others, back in the same inn when the journey is complete. It is part of the appeal of *The Canterbury Tales* that the journey is, in fact, never complete. The feast is never over. When Dryden said of this extraordinary smorgasbord of human experience, 'Here is God's plenty,' he used a word that is most often found in the context of food. We say there was plenty to eat and there is plenty more if you are still hungry. If we are asked if we have had enough, we might say we've had plenty. Chaucer has never had enough. His world is a feast of many flavours. He is a writer who sharpens our appetite for it.

CHAPTER 36

How to Live

Seneca, *On the Shortness of Life* (c. 55 CE)

Trivial ideas sound better in Latin. It's one thing that keeps the language alive so many centuries after the last gladiator bit the dust. Latin is not great for discussing computer problems, rocket science or dry-cleaning. But when it comes to lofty sentiments such as 'do your best' or 'seek the truth', there is nothing better. It is one thing to say 'overcome adversity' and another to pronounce *per ardua ad astra*. Latin clichés never sound like clichés. They sound like part of a coat of arms. My favourite Latin dictum, vouchsafed to me by an elderly nun, is *omni quique proprius stercus bene olet*. It means 'to each person, their own shit smells best.' I have always tried to live up to that. Latin is not all sunshine and light, however. It is responsible for both the ego and the CV, the status quo and the post-mortem. It also gave us alphabet soup: p.s., i.e., n.b., a.m., p.m., RIP, QED, etc.

The real thing that keeps Latin alive is its extraordinary literature. Its poetry and prose have been one of the places in my life where I have found shelter.

By the age of sixteen, most of my friends were creating the relationships that, in turn, would create their world. Some of the most important were with places. These included sporting grounds, music venues, record shops, burger joints and pubs which, in those days, were more inclined to turn a blind eye to the question of age. The memory of these locations can still allow my contemporaries to let slip the preoccupations of middle age, a bit like stepping out of a heavy coat. Love needs a someone. But it also needs a somewhere.

One of my somewheres was Tyrell's Bookshop on the Pacific Highway at Crows Nest in Sydney, just up the road from the Chinese Lantern, where you could get all you could eat for five dollars with a choice of rice or chips to go with the sweet-and-sour. If I stayed on the bus that took me home from school for an extra ten minutes, I could sneak a visit to Tyrell's and vanish from the world for a short time, becoming invisible among the tight shelves and piles of books, magazines and general clutter. It was a safe place for me in an otherwise confusing world.

I still have books I bought in those years. Looking at them now, I realise that I must have been an insufferable nerd because many of them are Latin texts. I loved them and the immunity they gave me from reality.

These little books are still full of notes and annotations which, along with that obsessive sticky tape, allow me to meet my sixteen-year-old self all over again, an anxious kid looking both for ways to matter and places to hide. I loved Latin because I thought it was such a compact language, perfect for superior beings such as myself who liked to pass judgement with a terse phrase that still allowed them to keep arm's length from whatever it was they were judging. Latin can create the illusion you can control the world, nail it down with a few words, and I needed that illusion.

One of the books I took home from Tyrell's for the princely sum of a dollar was *Latin Elegy, Lyric and Epigram* (1970) edited by three teachers, Dale, Thompson and Craddock, each of whom seemed to me to have been alive when Ovid was sent into exile on the Black Sea. But in such a musty tome I found this line:

> *Omnia mors poscit. Lex est, non poena, perire.*
> Death owns everything. It's the law, not a
> punishment, to perish.

The author was Seneca the younger (4 BCE to 65 CE), so called to distinguish him from his father, Seneca the elder. Seneca's only known child, a boy, didn't live long. This was sad, but it did solve the problem of finding a name for him other than Seneca the Yet Younger. There was something in those words of Seneca that braced my soul's palate, a bit like a first taste of mouldy cheese. I loved the affectation of bleakness. It was certainly easier than dealing with people. I was a cheerless youth and Seneca was a handy accessory:

> *Omnia tempus edax despascitur.*
> Time is the omnivore that eats everything.

I was wrong both about myself and about Seneca.

Seneca, a philosopher and dramatist, is one of those people remembered as much for his death as for his life. His former pupil, the emperor Nero, ordered him to commit suicide when he was associated with a plot to kill him. Seneca may not have been the first teacher who wanted to kill a student but in this case he was probably innocent. The strange thing is that, after a lifetime of fragile health, Seneca proved almost impossible to kill. He survived several attempts, including wrist-slashing, leg-slashing and poison, before he was suffocated in steam. He would have given the monk Rasputin a run for his money and Seneca had no shortage of that, having lined his pockets with the proceeds of living at close quarters to power. Despite his philosophical protestations about the transient nature of worldly existence, he was happy to make a buck out of it while it lasted.

It would be better to remember Seneca for a work of witty prose called *On the Shortness of Life*. Appropriately for its title, it is brief. It was written in the same decade and the same place as another succinct work, the Gospel According to St Mark. The two pieces bear comparison, not least because both were written partly to deal with the impact of a destructive political leader, namely Nero. Nero only became emperor through the connivance of his mother, Agrippina, the sister of Caligula. He was one of those whose personal insecurity led to violence. Both Seneca and the Markan community deal with the inevitability of suffering and the place of fear in coping with it. Mark asks people to hold on and endure. Seneca asks them to let go because it will all soon be over. You'd expect it to be the other way around. Seneca and Mark confront the depravity of a ravenous ego with works of extraordinary self-possession.

On the Shortness of Life was written over a century before Marcus Aurelius's famous meditations. It is a bijou from a misunderstood philosophical movement known as Stoicism, a brand for which Marcus Aurelius is the usual poster boy. These days, a person is described as 'stoic' when they play a game of football with a broken arm. A better word for this would be 'stupid'. Stoicism is not about the denial of real pain, real anxiety, real grief or, indeed, anything real. It is about using the mind not to change reality but to deal with it by placing it in a broader context. Naturally, this has the effect of changing reality, because we are part of that reality and if we change ourselves, we change the world, at least in a small way.

Seneca could well have written a book called *On the Shortness of Breath*. He spent a lifetime battling against his uncooperative lungs: he had severe asthma and bronchitis. Coughing and wheezing became his calling cards. He spent a good part of his adult life a few heartbeats from power and one short breath from oblivion. He existed on a knife edge. His philosophy and drama both reflect this.

He grew up in what is now called Spain, developing a passion for rhetoric and the well-honed phrase under the influence of his father. He spent years in Egypt, trying to find a better climate for his lungs. He was later exiled by the emperor Claudius to the island of Corsica on the trumped-up charge of adultery. It is hard to believe the lean and ascetical Seneca having the wind to get up to any such mischief. But Claudius's wife needed him out of the way.

Nero's mother brought him back when she wanted her son educated. Seneca may have been an excellent teacher but this doesn't mean that Nero learnt anything from him, certainly as far as morality is concerned. Seneca was trying to extricate himself from the emperor's circles when he wrote *On the Shortness of Life*.

The book argues that we are not given a short life but that we 'make it short' through all the unnecessary things we do to fritter away our time. He notes that people who are careful with their money and property are happy just to give their time away. He sees this as an obvious contradiction. 'You are living as if destined to live for ever; your own frailty never occurs to you.' Then he challenges us:

> Learning how to live takes a whole life and, which may surprise you more, it takes a whole life to learn how to die…You must not think a person has lived long because they have grey hair and wrinkles: they have not lived long, just existed long. For suppose you should think that a person had had a long voyage who had been caught in a raging storm as they left the harbour, and carried hither and thither and driven round and round in a circle by the rage of the opposing winds? They did not have a long voyage, just a long tossing about.

Seneca says 'the preoccupied find life very short' and is impatient with people who put things off and 'spend their lives in organising their lives'. The reason for this is 'the whole future lies in uncertainty: get living now.' He distinguishes between a life of leisure, which is great, and idle preoccupation, which is awful. If a person goes to their country house and thinks about the arrangement of their furniture or something like that, then they are prisoners of their own pettiness. 'Do you call people leisured who divide their time between the comb and the mirror?...It would be tedious to mention those who have spent all their lives playing draughts or balls or cooking themselves in the sun.' The answer is simple:

> Of all people only those are at leisure who make time for philosophy, only those are really alive. For they not only keep a good watch over their own lifetimes, but they annex every age to theirs...We are excluded from no age; we have access to them all...None of these will force you to die, but all will teach you how to die. None of them will exhaust your years, but each will contribute their years to yours.

In other words, if you read *On the Shortness of Life*, your span of years is suddenly around two thousand.

CHAPTER 37

Monstrous Strange

Herodotus, First paragraph of
The Histories (fifth century BCE)

You can read the whole thing if you like. You won't get bored. Herodotus's *Histories* is said to be the first book of non-fiction ever written, a problematic claim because large parts of it are so gloriously improbable. The word Herodotus uses for 'history' is actually more like 'enquiry', or even 'research', an apt reminder of what historians really do or should be doing. They are tedious when they only want to prove a point, however close that point may be to their heart. They are fascinating when they find things out and expose those things to uncomfortable questions such as 'Why?' and 'What did this lead to?' and 'Did anyone really think this was a good idea at the time?'

Herodotus and Socrates, who knew each other in the relatively small world of Athens in the fifth century BCE, were two very different kettles of fish. They both unsettled the world with endless questions, but Socrates used questions to distil the world to its essence. His habit of mind was sceptical. Herodotus, on the other hand, was credulous. He used questions to celebrate the complexity of the world. His *Histories* is full of digressions and back alleys and the most sublime irrelevancies. Anyone who has ever lost track of the time when online will be right at home in Herodotus. He is not a historian for whom one thing leads to another. For him, anything can lead in dozens of directions. He was as much interested in links as in cause and effect.

Herodotus had a big story and used over twenty-five thousand lines to tell it. In many ways, it's a story whose effects we live with every day, arguably as much as we live with the impact of World War I or World War II. In the first half of the fifth century BCE, a Greek alliance fought off a planned takeover from the empire of Persia, based where Iran happens to be today. The smart money was on Persia but the Greeks held them back. Had the result gone the other way, the extraordinary flourishing of thought and culture in fifth-century Greece would most likely never have happened. There would have been no Socrates, Plato or Aristotle. None of the great theatre of that time. None of the ideas that became the raw material out of which our civilisation was built. Instead, we would have just had more battlefields and more dead bodies, and God knows history has had plenty of those. Herodotus is great partly because he had a great topic. Battles such as Marathon and Thermopylae are on his bailiwick.

He is also great because of the way he dealt with his material. Nothing was beyond his interest and it is not surprising that he has also been considered the first ethnographer. His researches led him to tell stories about flying snakes, snakes whose young eat their way out of their mothers in order to be born and snakes with horns. He also encounters ants the size of cats, men that eat other men, women who eat other women, men with the heads of dogs and men without heads at all. Indeed, when Shakespeare's Othello wants to woo the divine Desdemona, he impresses her with tales of travel in a world that could only have been charted by Herodotus (see Chapter 34).

Herodotus is also a connoisseur of human eccentricity. By the second or third page of his vast epic, he puts the story on hold so he can tell us about Candaules, the king of Lydia, who has given his name to a particular sexual proclivity. Candaules believes he has the most beautiful wife in the world and insists that his steward, Gyges, hide himself in his bedchamber so he can see the queen in the nude and judge for himself. When the queen finds out, she says that Gyges can only restore her honour by either killing himself or killing the king and taking her hand in marriage. Gyges takes the second option and thus becomes king.

Herodotus enjoys the grim humour of history. He tells of a practical joke played by Queen Nitocris, who left an inscription on her tomb that any king of Babylon who was short of money could find some handy cash in her coffin. King Darius can't resist. But when he defiles the queen's grave, he only finds another note accusing him of greed. No reader could doubt that Herodotus loved his work.

Nevertheless, if you only have time to read the first few lines of Herodotus, you will find a description of the historian's craft that has never, in my experience, been bettered. Here is Tom Holland's translation:

> Herodotus, from Halicarnassus, here displays his enquiries, that human achievement may be spared the ravages of time, and that everything great and astounding, and all the glory of those exploits which served to display Greeks and Barbarians alike to such effect, be kept alive—and additionally, and most importantly, to give the reason they went to war.

The first thing to think about is how similar and yet different this is from the opening of Homer's *Iliad* (see Chapter 38), a work which Herodotus actually gave its name. Homer also says that he is going to explain the causes of war. But *The Iliad* looks for explanations both beyond the human realm and inside it. The work is inspired by the goddess of song. It asks of the participants in the tragic Trojan War: 'Which of the gods was it that made them quarrel?'

Herodotus, by way of contrast, starts with his own name, and to ensure there is no mistaking his identity, adds his birthplace as well, a city on the coast of what is now western Turkey. It might say something about the open-mindedness of Herodotus that he was born between Persia and Greece. At all events, this is history as the creation of an author, an individual whose personality and nimble wit infuses every page. It is not an anonymous official version. There is a creative imagination at work and that means there is somebody taking responsibility.

The second thing is Herodotus's motivation. He writes so that 'human achievement may be spared the ravages of time.'

So, like a good friend of Socrates, he is writing in the face of mortality, pushing back against the great oblivion to which most of us will be eventually consigned. He wants the 'great and astounding' achievements of all people, not just the Greeks and certainly not just himself, to be 'kept alive'. This is a bid for immortality.

There are countless deaths in Herodotus, as there are in *The Iliad*. Readers of both works get lost in the enormous databank of names that each work enshrines, every name of a dead person, often brutally savaged without much dignity. But each work is powered by a belief in immortality. Homer finds it in the gods. This does not mean he believes in life after death. Those hundreds of Homeric dead bodies are well and truly dead, and that is how they are going to stay. But while alive, they were the playthings of a circus troupe of gods. Herodotus finds immortality in our present realm, in collective human memory. Later thinkers would come to realise that these two approaches are not so very different. Homer's gods are often intemperate little brats. Herodotus's humans are often larger than mere life.

Finally, in his first paragraph, Herodotus wants to show how two great civilisations, both of which has an energy he admires, came into conflict. All history needs to explain conflict. The first paragraph of the first book of history ever written seems to understand what the job was all about. The centuries that followed have shown just how tough that job was going to be.

CHAPTER 38

Souvlaki

Homer, Book 24 of *The Iliad* (eighth century BCE)

The humble souvlaki has a venerable place in history. It is the pivot on which turns one of the great moments in all literature.

By the final chapter of Homer's *Iliad*, an epic about the Trojan War and much else besides, the whole world is exhausted. It is uncomfortable to have reached this nadir so early in the history of western storytelling. *The Iliad* takes us right back to our origins. It took shape more than 2,700 years ago, long before Socrates, The Bible and even the Rolling Stones. But its origins lay back even further, and scholars have approached *The Iliad* a bit like an archaeological site. Buried within it are all sorts of words, phrases and descriptions that provide a sort of time capsule of pre-history. Adam Nicolson, author of *The Mighty Dead: Why Homer Matters* (2014), has described the way in which Homer enshrines words that date from before the Greeks came to Greece, something that probably happened around 2000 BCE. It is a window on a civilisation from much further north and much further back:

> Homer is full of half-buried memories of that northern past, and his recollections hint at another non-Mediterranean world, far from water, far from cities, land-locked, dominated by an enormous sky, horse-rich, focused on flocks and herds and the meat they provide, violent, mobile and heroic...That other northern place lurks as a kind of murmured, ancestral layer, a subconscious.

Nicolson points out that a great deal of the language of Homer is so old that not even Homer would have been able to read Homer. This is at least some comfort to those who have faced the challenging task of translating Homer. But wait a moment. This statement assumes that we can identify who Homer was. In fact, we know virtually nothing about him or her. Legend holds that Homer was blind. But Homer may equally have been a name used for convenience to describe the source of an experience of storytelling and song which lies far beyond the control of any one individual.

Reading Homer, you know that its origins lie far away. It comes from a distant time and place; it is elevated beyond the petty daily grind. Of all the countless acts of brilliance in the hundreds of episodes of the TV program *The Simpsons*, none was ever more brilliant than to call the main character Homer. Homer Simpson is the anti-hero with no grand overarching narrative in his life. He is in charge of security at a nuclear plant, which means he may very well hold the future of the world in his clumsy and accident-prone hands. But Homer Simpson has no capacity to stop and wonder what that might mean, which is why he is so excruciatingly funny. He is everything the original Homer was not.

It is a wonder that we have *The Iliad* and *The Odyssey*, Homer's other epic, at all. *The Iliad* has been in print since the fifteenth century CE. It would have been in print even longer except for the fact that it was around before printing was invented. Before the fifteenth century, *The Iliad* existed in manuscripts on paper. Long before that, it may have existed in manuscripts written on hide. If you have encountered people struggling to breathe with diphtheria, you will not be surprised to learn that the name of the illness originates in the Greek word for 'leather'. In ancient times, some Greeks used the same word for 'book'. Before any written version, *The Iliad* was passed from mouth to ear, handed across communities and generations in an oral form. An oral tradition is less fragile than commonly supposed. Storytellers had a sacred trust. They did not feel free to tinker with their material. Even so, *The Iliad* is a long way from its source.

The Iliad did not survive for so long because it was some kind of light entertainment or even historical saga. It survived because communities found the power of the story necessary for their own survival. *The Iliad* is still an extraordinary force. It is worth wrestling with in its entirety. But if you are running late for work, you can skip to the final extraordinary chapter, Chapter 24. There you will find a place for the souvlaki that would satisfy even Homer Simpson, a man with a significant appetite for junk food.

From the outset, *The Iliad* lets us know that its focus is anger. The opening word of Robert Fagles' contemporary translation is 'Rage'. The first word of the eighteenth-century translation by the poet Alexander Pope is 'Wrath'. It's hard to miss the message. *The Iliad* speaks to every war that was ever fought and to every scene of domestic violence. It is an enormous structure because it needs to carry such a heavy burden. It deals with the anger and violence, particularly male anger and male violence, that have driven human history into countless tragedies. I don't know if anybody has ever counted the number of dead bodies in *The Iliad*. It would be thousands. One of the reasons people find *The Iliad* heavy weather and much less fluid than *The Odyssey* is that the epic constantly interrupts itself to let us know who these dead people are. We get their names and those of their parents and grandparents and siblings and comrades and, if pizzas had been invented, we would have got the name of the delivery guy as well. The book is carpeted with the kind of detail that a modern editor would sweep away in the interests of clean storytelling. But, for Homer, all these people, many of whom die in gruesome circumstances, never stop being people. Homer has no sense of life beyond the grave. Their immortality is in the telling of human history.

From page one, however, we find that the particular anger is that of the great warrior Achilles, the son of a divine mother, Thetis, and a mortal father, Peleus. Achilles is offstage for significant parts of *The Iliad*. But his anger is the poem's engine room.

By Book 24, the Greeks have been camped out on the plains beyond Troy for ten years; the Trojans have been stuck behind walls. Eventually, to cut a long story short, Achilles, who is supposed to be brave, allows his best friend, Patroclus, to do battle with the Trojan hero, Hector. Patroclus even wears Achilles' armour so it looks from afar that Achilles is fighting. Hector dies and Achilles is furious. His anger has a tectonic force. Of course, some of this anger should be directed against himself for allowing Patroclus to take the heat and make Achilles look cowardly. But Achilles is cross with Hector. He fights Hector and kills him. Mere killing is not enough. Revenge has not made him feel any better.

For twelve days, Achilles performs desecrations on the body of Hector. He drags the corpse of Hector around and around behind his chariot, no doubt hoping he could come back to life so he could kill him again. And again. Hector's nobility means his remains are somehow protected. Despite such treatment, they do not deteriorate in any way. The body is miraculously protected. The stronger Achilles appears in his rage, the more impotent he appears. He can't sleep. He loses his appetite. His food has no taste.

Then a curious thing happens. Priam, the king of Troy, steps down from the regal trappings of his position to assume an unfamiliar role, that of a father. His wife, Hecuba, the mother of nineteen of Priam's children, protests loudly. It is too risky. They have already lost too many of their children in this stupid war. Indeed, Priam has lost fifty sons in battle. Is she going to lose a husband as well? But Priam is adamant. He believes he is following the prompting of the gods, who have instructed him to take a ransom to the Greeks and humbly ask if he can bring back the body of Hector. He becomes a human being, making his way to the tent of mighty Achilles to seek the remains of his son. He is accompanied on the journey by a simple wagon owner and guided by Hermes, the most mercurial of all the gods, the one who knows no boundaries.

Priam expects to be killed. But he has not reckoned on the fact that the whole world is now tired of conflict and aggression. It is heartily sick of the macho posturing and muscle flexing of men. It needs something different and humility breaks the deadlock. Achilles has been trapped in a pathetically small image of masculinity. Priam reminds him of his own father, whom he has not seen for ten years. Priam's defencelessness gets past all of Achilles' defences. Achilles is relieved.

At the key moment of *The Iliad*, one of the pivotal points of all literature, Achilles offers Priam a souvlaki: lamb, roasted on a rotisserie spit, cut into pieces and served in bread. Admittedly, Homer makes no mention of garlic sauce. But both men taste food again for the first time. They begin the long journey home from their grief. They become friends. The humble souvlaki achieved as much as did any imperial banquet in history.

CHAPTER 39

My Tears Have Become My Bread

A taste of the Torah, the Bible, the Qur'an

I like to be the first person awake in my house. With three teenage children, this isn't hard, especially at the weekend. I love to get a cup of coffee and look out the window. Most of the time, I will allow my Bible to fall open at Psalm 63. After years of training, it does this with a mind of its own.

This isn't just any Bible. At the time my father died in 1979, when I was a month short of my eighteenth birthday, I stuck to my foolhardy plan to head off and join the Jesuit order, committing myself to a life of poverty, chastity, obedience and, as it turned out, joyous eccentricity. Mum knew I was in flight but she was stoic. We had been told to buy a certain edition of the Bible to take with us and Mum wanted to give that to me as a gift. She borrowed a copy to make sure she got the right one in the city. So, on a hot summer's day, she dragged a bag with not one but two copies of this hefty tome through the streets of Sydney. The handle of the bag tore, so then she had to hold it to her like a baby, refusing all offers of help.

When she got home, she wrote in the front: 'To dear Michael. In loving memory of your darling father, Gregory McGirr. Much love always, Mum. XO.'

The Bible has many pages and I have read most of them, some many times. But Psalm 63 is the place at which every new day starts for me:

> My soul is thirsting for you,
> My flesh is longing for you,
> A land, parched, weary and waterless.

After so many years, I have not exhausted these ancient words, nor tired of them, nor given up on the search they celebrate, nor yet properly understood the vulnerability they call for. All these things are part of what makes the words sacred. They are attributed to the notoriously opportunistic King David, but who knows where they come from. The Psalms are said to be so beautiful because the predatory King David had every reason to be humble. Sure enough, the literary and historical search for the roots of these words, and many like them, is fascinating and I have often enjoyed the intellectual spadework of scriptural study, especially when it is peppered with rare linguistic spice. But nothing is sacred because it keeps academics amused. Scripture is sacred because of the life of the community that is nurtured by it. Just mouthing the words of Psalm 63 does something for me about watering the parched and weary land to which they refer. I guess by this stage of the game I could say them by heart but they belong in a book, which I treat with affection, even though it is frustrating and elusive and even though it is abused by people who want to ink their egos between the lines. A sacred text is always vulnerable. That is another part of what makes it sacred.

> On my bed I think of you,
> I meditate on you all night long,
> For you have always helped me.

~

My Year 10 class studies Islam, one of the most formative influences in the world that my students will inhabit and hopefully improve. I have a profound respect for Islam. Westerners, and especially western Christians, often fail to acknowledge the debt they owe to Islam, a tradition that had a huge role in bringing Europe through the Dark Ages and into the Renaissance. I tell students and anyone else who expresses a mindless contempt for Islam that if they truly feel that way then they should have the strength of their convictions and stop using Arabic numerals. The reason we use Arabic numbers in the first place is that they embody a philosophical concept that was inaccessible to Roman numerals and that, indeed, was threatening to medieval Christianity. That is the idea of zero, the representation of nothing, the articulation of the void.

Zero is a wonderful image of eternity. If you try to divide anything by zero, you have an experience of both the eternal and the absurd right before your eyes, beneath the tip of a cheap pencil. Zero is a perfect circle with nothing to enclose: it has neither beginning nor end. Christians sometimes scratch their heads when Muslims speak of the impossibility of creating visual images of the divine. Mosques don't have statues or pictures. But zero is, in fact, not a bad representation of the sacred.

Christianity tells stories; Islam finds designs, patterns, mosaics. These communities should love each other. Often enough it looks like there is zero chance of that. The prophet Muhammad was one of the liberators of history. It's a pity that a small number of his followers are hell-bent, to use the expression literally, on poisoning their own water. I wouldn't want Christianity judged by the actions of the Ku Klux Klan.

I offer my students a more sympathetic account of the mysticism of Islam than they are likely to get from the media at large. We visit mosques. On one occasion, an imam explained the beliefs of Islam, then quickly moved on to a range of herbal cosmetics and medicines which he was selling, clearly as part of a pyramid scheme. There was comfort in knowing that dodgy practices could cross religious boundaries.

Another mosque, in a northern suburb, occupied a former showroom on top of nondescript shops. It was so plain that, looking for a minaret or a dome shining in the sun, we were twenty minutes late. The imam spoke simply about the need for community and belonging and a moral structure for living, precisely the messages we try to impart to the students on our side of the tracks. Someone asked about 'jihad'. The imam explained that it has nothing to do with violence.

The word means 'struggle'. He hoped that all of us were engaged in the struggle to become the best people we could be. To achieve that, we needed both ancient wisdom and a contemporary community. It was important not to struggle *against* but to struggle *with*.

'Why do we have to take off our shoes?' asked one student.

'It shows respect. Respect is one of the crutches we need to help us learn reverence.'

It was an interesting image.

'No one runs to God. We only get there on crutches.'

~

In another mosque, Sherene Hassan, the founder of Melbourne's Islamic Museum of Australia, tells us that there are about 6,200 verses in the Qur'an and less than a dozen suggest any kind of violence. Sometimes the Qur'an pacifies its biblical antecedents, such as in the way it retells the story of the world's first murder, that of Abel by his brother Cain, an event that does not record history but, like so much in sacred texts, is more focussed on creating a future. The Qur'an's version ends with the words: 'the one who kills a soul…it is as if he killed the whole of mankind.'

Imam Mehmet Salih Dogan told us about his journey from Turkey and how he was proud of the work his wife was doing as a midwife in the enormous public hospital just across the road from where his community was trying to build a new mosque. 'She helps bring life into the world. That is what Islam is all about. Bringing life to the world.'

The imam introduced us to a Year 10 student from the local high school, a young man in a cheap tracksuit. He wore his baseball hat backwards. We had to remove our shoes, but hats were acceptable. This chap had already committed a third of the Qur'an to memory. In Arabic. It poured out of him as if it was too much for a single body to contain.

'Wow,' said Shaun, one of our group, seldom short of a word. 'That's incredible.'

The boy explained that the word Qur'an meant 'recitation': it is a work that doesn't yield its magic on the page, but only in being heard aloud within a community. His life's goal was to memorise the entire book.

The Prophet Muhammad could neither read nor write, a fact often mentioned to support the belief that the Qur'an is divinely inspired. A better proof, in my view, is not so much how a book was created as what it, in turn, creates. All of my students were struck dumb by the commitment of this young man to the Qur'an and to the Arabic well from which it was drawn. I was having a holy struggle of my own to get some of them to read the fifty small pages of Mark's Gospel, let alone commit any of it to memory.

Modern education is prone to neglect the importance of memory. This does not mean rote learning. It means taking something important into the fabric of your being. People who have memorised great poetry will speak about this. So will actors who have performed Shakespeare and other major texts, as well as pianists and singers who have remembered breathtaking works. Such things shape the memory and in turn shape the person. The memory is like a muscle. It needs to do heavy lifting to gain its strength and power. The act of memory requires humility; you have to surrender yourself.

The great traditions of wisdom are inaccessible without it. Apps are handy. You can carry a thousand works of literature in your phone. But they will never be part of you.

The students always ask the same question. 'Why do we have to remove our shoes?' Shaun queried the imam.

'Because when I smell your feet,' he replied. 'I know we share the same humanity.'

We all laughed.

'And if we share the same humanity,' he continued, 'we can only share the same God.'

~

My favourite line in the Bible is 'my tears have become my bread, by night, by day', which is in Psalm 42. These words help me to understand my least-favourite line, which is also probably the most important. This is the one that contains the last words spoken by Jesus in Mark's Gospel as he dies in horrendous circumstances: 'My God, My God, why have you abandoned me?'

Mark's Gospel was written thirty years after the events it describes, on the other side of the known world, in a language that none of the people in the story would have spoken. But these words are included in Aramaic, a hint that they are a genuine memory for the community, handed on by the women who witnessed the death of Jesus after his male friends had made themselves scarce. They are the same words as the first line of Psalm 22, which Jesus evidently knew so well that, as he was stripped of every human dignity, it was still part of him.

~

For at least four decades, Br Bernie, the prior of the Cistercian Abbey at Tarrawarra (see Chapter 16), has been part of a community that recites all one hundred and fifty Psalms every week. They start each day at 4 a.m. This is the time when we are all most vulnerable, and vulnerability is the door to the inner life of any sacred text and to any kind of intimacy, especially with the divine. There are times in life to be strong. There are just as many times not to be. Bernie says that the Psalms are like old friends. Their mood can change for him from one week to the next.

~

At my father's funeral, we sang Psalm 139:

> If I asked darkness to cover me,
> And light to become night around me,
> That darkness would not be dark to you,
> Night would be as light as day.

Parts of scripture such as this are like a pebble in my shoe, constantly reminding me that there is more to life than just me and more to time than a linear progression of past, present and future. They prevent me striding around in my world, comfortable in what Shakespeare, in *Measure for Measure*, calls 'a little brief authority'.

Encounters with the poor are the same. There might be reasons to think of community-service programs as a kind of tokenism. There might be even more reasons to think carefully about taking young people to the developing world to take part in what is sometimes known as voluntourism, a bit of work whose main outcome is to make the traveller feel okay about themselves and their part of an unjust world. I once visited a school in which students were reporting at assembly about a trip they had made to Cambodia. As part of the visit, the young people had helped to repair and paint a small hall for their host community.

'I had never seen such poverty,' said one girl. 'I had never imagined people lived like that. But we knew we were making a difference. We left feeling good.'

This addiction to feeling good is a problem. Surely if we ask our young people to experience something troubling, we should want them to feel troubled. The soul of education is being strangled by a monster called anxiety. Real education is all about risk. It is a risk, after all, to learn how to read, because reading will inevitably bring ideas into your life that upset your apple cart. If we expose our young to something bad and orchestrate the situation so they end up feeling good, we are allowing them to hide inside a lie that says their life is all about themselves. For me, the greatest challenge of education is to lead young people to a place of such vulnerable strength that they can surrender their ego and find the freedom that lies beyond its grasp in lives of service and gritty love.

Nevertheless, an experience of how most of the world lives can transform lives. Aged twenty-three, I was sent by the Jesuit order to live for three weeks in a slum in Jakarta. The order thought I'd had a pretty cushy life up till then and they were right. That experience has been a pebble in my shoe for well over thirty years. It is uncomfortable but I am glad it is there. I would love the students I teach to experience this.

So I was more than grateful to have been able to visit East Africa with a group of young people in 2014. We were unable to land in Nairobi because of security concerns. So we had to take a minibus overland from Dar es Salaam, in Tanzania, to the place we were visiting in Kenya. It was a distance of nine hundred kilometres on some rough roads.

The bus was a broken-winded old hack. It had a fluoro sign at the front bearing its name: *Thanks Dear*. The driver, whose name was Goodluck, turned the key in the ignition and the engine gave an irritable cough as though it was annoyed at being disturbed. Eventually, it spluttered into life. The vehicle seemed to have poor lungs. It was a smoker. Clouds billowed from its exhaust.

A quick look inside and we began counting seats. There was no roof rack. We'd be lucky if we could squeeze all our gear into the back row. After that, there wouldn't be enough places for everyone. Goodluck's co-pilot, Bahati, appeared and everyone smiled and shook hands but I couldn't help thinking that he'd need another seat. Then two more helpers turned up, as well. It was going to be a very crowded trip.

'Maybe we should think of running,' said Roland.

Minibuses provoke claustrophobia in some people but this was not Roland's problem. He had grown up in the back of a Toyota LandCruiser. There were seven kids in his family, including a young cousin who, for various reasons, had grown up with them and was as much part of the fabric of life as any sibling. They were used to squashing in. It was part of life.

No, Roland was thinking of running because, like Timas Harik (see Chapter 23), who was a couple of years older than him, he found freedom in running. He had run eight hundred metres in 1.54. A bit slower than Timas but no jog. At the big interschool athletics competition the year before, Roland took the final leg of the 4 x 800 metres relay. It was a tough race. Another member of his team was shortly to run an Olympic qualifying time for the distance but the competition was equally as good. Unfortunately, Roland's relay team came second by an ankle. He can replay every step of that race from memory.

'Were you disappointed?'

'I was. It took me a long, long time to get over it.'

'Really. How long did it take?'

Roland thought carefully. 'I reckon it took a couple of hours.'

Now he was ready to run not eight hundred metres but eight hundred kilometres. 'I reckon we can do it,' he said.

He showed me a tattoo on his hip that he had recently acquired. It said, 'Do not let your hearts be troubled—John 14.1.'

'It's my favourite verse,' he said.

I told him that a phrase such as 'don't worry', or 'do not be afraid', or 'do not let your hearts be troubled', occurs in the Bible on three hundred and sixty-five occasions, one for each day of the year. Dealing with anxiety is one of the great themes of all sacred texts.

We got the bus and it was fine.

~

A sacred text will close itself off if it is read in anger. It will lock its doors against those who use it to prove a point. It will turn a deaf ear to the opinions of those who know what it means in the first place. It will mock those who think that they are the centre of the universe. It will scorn the self-righteous.

But it will open itself to a mind and heart that can be honest about the rough and tumble of life. It will flower in laughter and pain. Psalm 131 says:

> Truly I have set my soul
> In silence and peace
> A weaned child on its mother's breast
> Even so is my soul.

~

One of the biblical stories that fascinates me most concerns a risky traveller, the prophet Elijah, a figure revered in Judaism, Christianity and Islam. Elijah stood up to King Ahab, who gave his name to the central character of *Moby-Dick* (see Chapter 28). After a flight of forty days and forty nights through the wilderness, during which time things got so bad that Elijah huddled under a furze bush and wished he were dead, the prophet reaches Mt Horeb. There he takes shelter in a cave for the night. A mighty wind goes past, then there is an earthquake and then a fire. God is present in none of these dramatic happenings. But then there is a gentle breeze and that feels more like God. Elijah covers his face and comes out of his cave.

CHAPTER 40

The Way Home

Lao Tzu, *Tao Te Ching* (c. sixth century BCE)

There are books that you fall into in the same way as you fall into a lifeboat.

When the sales are in full swing, it could take half an hour to drive to the vast shopping centre fifteen minutes' walk from our house. Even on a quiet day, the centre will have sixty thousand visitors, all armed with credit cards, all looking for something. One day I was sitting there having spent a thousand dollars on school shoes and camping equipment when a crane arrived and delivered a real live palm tree into the middle of the place. It was at least ten metres tall; the roots were neatly packaged in a ball. Once, people travelled to the tropics. Now, they can be delivered by truck.

The mall is not my idea of a wild Saturday night. But one winter's evening, my son Jacob, then aged twelve, reported that he could not do his school project because the screen on one of his devices was broken. The beauty of the mall is, of course, that you can have all your frustrations and disappointments conveniently located under a single roof. The people who sold us the device, along with an extended warranty, didn't want to know us because the warranty did not cover screens nor, it seemed to me, any other part of the gadget that was likely to break. The original packaging may have been covered against tears in the cardboard in the event that it was eaten by a dog, as long as the dog was registered with three councils and desexed. But we had thrown out the box in the mistaken belief that the contents were more important. There is nothing finer than fine print.

We then went to the mother store of the manufacturer, where squads of eager helpers of every age, race, size and piercing preference were available to offer advice. They all wore identical blue T-shirts, which had the effect of making them all look different from each other. The customers, on the other hand, all looked the same. Mostly they were middle-aged men with children whose broken screens stood between them and academic success.

We were helped by Dan, who happened to be a recent graduate from the school where I worked. We immediately got talking about my friend and colleague Chris Straford, who had died not long before (see Chapter 14). Dan reminisced about the Sunday evenings when he went with Chris to a local bakery to pick up unsold bread and deliver it to a number of communities and relief centres in the inner city. It was clear that this connection with struggling people had touched Dan more than all the gadgets in the world. There isn't a website or an app that can do the same thing.

But none of this meant that Dan could help us with the cracked screen. We were referred to one of the numerous repair booths around the centre. The first one offered to fix our small problem for $349. The second one for $300. The third for $245. The farther we walked from the mother store, the cheaper it got.

'I think we should take it to the third one,' said Jacob.

Actually, I didn't think we needed to take it to any of them. He was clearly a genius already. Further education was unnecessary.

I was not in the best frame of mind when we finally found a table in one of the many food courts to wait for the repair. A food court is by no means a court of justice, although they can provide work for lawyers. We were surrounded by all the cuisines of the world, cheerfully presented in warmer trays. You could eat from any continent of the world and practically any country. Yet every meal was available with Coke.

I allowed Jacob and his sister to wander for a while to kill time. I love that expression. Time will eventually kill us all, so it's nice to be able to get in first.

As I waited for their return, I decided to poke my head in a nearby bookstore, part of a large chain, to find something to read so I, too, could kill time. Here I found another student, Marcel, from my philosophy class. I asked him to point me to the philosophy section. He didn't know where it was. Clearly, I had stirred in him an insatiable curiosity about the subject. On the other hand, he may well have responded that the whole establishment was dedicated to philosophy, especially the philosophy of cooking, investment advice and sports biography.

'Let's find it together,' I suggested.

We did.

It consisted of a single book. The *Tao Te Ching* by Lao Tzu.

'Just what I was looking for,' I said.

'Oh, that's great,' said Marcel, smiling broadly. He may have been happy to have served a customer. It was also just possible that if I had found what I wanted, his teacher would soon leave the store.

In fact, I was completely unfamiliar with the book. But it cost less than a plate of food from one of the scores of warmers in the food court, so I decided it would be better to waste my money on indigestible literature than indigestible food.

I returned to the food court where this slender volume, translated from the Chinese in 1964 and still lurking in a book supermarket, swallowed me up.

It was like finding a lifeboat to rescue me from the waves of colour and noise pounding on every side in the mall.

Here were eighty-one short meditations that were composed in another time and place. Lao Tzu, whoever he or she may have been, was older than Confucius and a contemporary of Socrates.

It was the perfect riposte to the seas of consumerism rising around me. It was a call to sanity, simplicity and a rich sense of irony in the face of human attempts to be too serious. The final meditation says:

Truthful words are not beautiful; beautiful words are not truthful. Good words are not persuasive; persuasive words are not good. He who knows has no wide learning; he who has wide learning does not know. The sage does not hoard. Having bestowed all he has on others, he has yet more: having given all he has to others, he is richer still.

I was happy. For ten bucks, I had got myself out of a hole and back on the earth. I was going home to set out on another adventure.

Jacob returned with a fresh screen and gave me a hug. 'You're a lifesaver,' he said.

I wanted to tell him about the things I read that had saved my life.

EPILOGUE
Words that Don't Come Easy

There is plenty to read in a cemetery. In the first few days of their last year at school, our senior students undertake their final retreat with us. As part of this experience, we take them for a while to the Melbourne General Cemetery, in Carlton North. The place is an overview of their diverse community.

They will find, for example, the grave of James Scullin, who was prime minister of Australia from 1929 to 1932, during the worst of the Great Depression. He is buried with his wife, Sarah. On his grave are written some of his own words: 'Justice and humanity demand interference whenever the weak are being crushed by the strong.' His grave sits among many ordinary graves. It is nothing like the monument to Roosevelt, America's Depression president.

Nearby is a moving plaque in recognition of 'mothers whose children were adopted and have subsequently died before reunion'. It says: 'but we were not separated in our hearts. Tomorrow we will sit with you and hear you laugh.'

There is also a Jewish section, which includes many survivors of Hitler's holocaust. They often say: may his or her dear soul rest in peace. There are many Italian, Greek and Chinese graves, as well. People of countless different origins end up here.

Beyond the Jewish section is a large stone obelisk to commemorate the unfortunate Burke and Wills. They undertook a legendary expedition to cross the Australian continent from north to south, setting out from a park a few hundred metres from this point. They died in the outback, at Coopers Creek in 1861, having more or less reached their goal, but they are still considered heroic failures. Heroism is more soothing to survivors than wretched bad luck. Just north of this monument is the grave of Sir Redmond Barry, a judge and for many years the chancellor of the University of Melbourne. Barry is best remembered as the man who sentenced Ned Kelly to the gallows. His grave reveals the irony that he died less than a fortnight after Kelly, making generations wonder about Kelly's threat to see the judge in the afterlife. Barry's grave says ambiguously: 'Deeply and universally regretted.' The Kelly clan were not part of that universe. Kelly himself is not here. His remains were interred in an unmarked grave. In the last few years, a small plaque has been added to remember Louisa Barrow, Barry's partner, who shared the same grave him for one hundred and thirty years without any acknowledgment. She was the mother of the great man's four children.

The cemetery includes the graves of some of the brothers whose order started our school. Among them is Br John Lynch, who died in 1921 at eighty-three. He was one of the four original brothers who arrived in Melbourne with Ambrose Treacy aboard the *Donald M'Kay* in 1868. The foursome needed to borrow money to pay their landing tax; they had nothing. When John Lynch died, fifty-three years later, the brothers had established a large network of schools of various kinds; from that point, their history became excruciatingly painful. As a young man, Lynch had been a fine horseman. But when he was helping children at St Vincent's Orphanage, he contracted a contagious form of ophthalmia and went blind. He shares the soil with Br Pat Daly, a Queenslander, who died of complications from appendicitis while he was on the staff of our school in 1947. Daly was only twenty-two years old. He was long remembered by his students for his youthful enthusiasm. The other brothers remembered the way he sat up late at night preparing lessons; in those days, he was sent into the classroom without much formal training.

These are just a few of the personalities in the cemetery. Our students look for the tree under which is buried Peter Lalor, the man who led the Eureka Stockade uprising in 1854. Equally important are the many hundreds of ordinary lives to which the headstones provide clues. There is the Robinson family who, in the 1870s, buried four of their children, James, Harry, Edith and Elsie, aged nineteen months, three years, six years and eleven months respectively. Venus Rennie's grave says simply that she is 'at rest' after twenty years of suffering; it doesn't say what kind of suffering. There is even a grave for a husband and wife who died fifty years apart: 'United at last.' Another grave contains two sisters, Jane and Helen Pigdon. One died in 1867 at the age of three. The other died in 1950 at the age of eighty-one.

We don't come here for a joyride into history, intriguing as all these stories may be. We come because of a book, *The Spiritual Exercises* by Ignatius of Loyola (1548), a distillation of his own life experience. St Ignatius was keen to help people who were making important decisions in their lives and few people fit that description as well as those starting their final year at school, wondering what the years after might hold, tossing up what course or career they might embark upon. Ignatius was insightful about decisions, not least because he had made a few bad ones. He believed that the mind is the safest point of entry to the heart: a decision-maker should start with a reasoned approach, considering the rational pros and cons of a particular course of action, and then move beyond that to a heartfelt approach, knowing that emotions can be liberated by reason. This is where the imagination plays a huge part in wise decision-making. He suggests, for example, that you should imagine a complete stranger in a similar situation to your own. What advice would you give them? More dramatically, he asks people to consider this moment from the perspective of the end of time. But most powerfully, he says that you should imagine looking back on this decision from the moment of your death. What would you wish you had done?

That is why we come to the cemetery, to ponder the mystery of life and the short lease we have of it. None of us have our lives freehold; we are part of a community which shapes us and which we, in turn, shape. Life can take an almost infinite number of possible directions. But all roads seem to lead to this one place. We will all reach the end of our days. What do we want to leave behind? Who will read our story in whatever form it may be written?

Literature is the work of people who are either dead or will be dead. Often enough, it is their leavings, their attempts to come to terms with the mystery that surrounds them on every side. Great literature always implies questions about the way we live and love. Reading has, at one level, saved my life.

At another level, it has helped me to surrender it, to put it in a wider context of human yearning.

The advice is often given to aspiring writers that they should write what they know. I go along with this to a limited extent. I think we should write at the very edge of what we know, pushing from the familiar into the unfamiliar, stumbling into areas where we are unsure if we can find words for what needs to be said. The main thing we need in our pencil case is honesty, the blood brother of humility. I am passionate about words that don't come easy, the ones that build real bridges between human beings rather than burying them under clichés and slogans. I love finding a shape for things that are shapeless or misshapen. I love the writer's faithful marriage to a reality beyond themselves. That is what has saved my life.

A WORD OF THANKS

I was once approached by a publisher to write a biography of a prominent figure and I considered the matter for a while. A wise woman told me that, before I signed on the dotted line, I should ask myself if I wanted to spend every hour of the next five years, day and night, with the subject of the proposed book. It turned out that I most certainly did not. He was a cardinal in the Catholic Church. I didn't warm to spending even my daylight hours with him, to say nothing of the ones after dark.

Literary biography is a world of its own. I have untold respect for those writers who are prepared to properly explore the universe of other writers. The experience of reading literary biography is vastly different from garnering a few facts from the internet. The best of the genre draws you close to the fascinating and elusive process of the writer's craft, something invisible to the eye but which leaves clues where patient understanding is prepared to find them. It can be thankless and exhausting work. Karen Lamb, whose biography of Thea Astley (see Chapter 10) is called *Inventing Her Own Weather*, told me that the book absorbed nearly all of her Sundays for eight years. It defies the imagination to work out what she earned as an hourly rate.

With this in mind, I would like to express my admiration and gratitude to the following hardy biographers. They hew wood and draw water in a cause that deserves better appreciation. Peter Ackroyd (Geoffrey Chaucer and Charles Dickens), Hugh Anderson and L. J. Blake (John Shaw Neilson), Karen Armstrong (Muhammad), Rosemary Ashton (George Eliot), Deidre Bair (Simone de Beauvoir), Juliet Barker (the Brontës), John Barnes (Joseph Furphy), Rosamund Bartlett (Leo Tolstoy), Mark Bostridge (Vera Brittain), Humphrey Carpenter (J. R. R. Tolkien), G. K. Chesterton (Geoffrey Chaucer), Andrew Delbanco (Herman Melville), Colin Duriez (J. R. R. Tolkien), David Edwards (John Donne), William Eggington (Miguel de Cervantes), Paul Elie (Flannery O'Connor, Dorothy Day and Thomas Merton), Monica Furlong (Thomas Merton), Elizabeth Gaskell (Charlotte Brontë), Victoria Glendinning (Leonard Woolf), Brad Gooch (Flannery O'Connor), Stephen Greenblatt (William Shakespeare), Cliff Hanna (John Shaw Neilson), Alexandra Harris (Virginia Woolf), Richard Holmes (Percy Bysshe Shelley), Kate Hennessy (Dorothy Day), Kathryn Hughes (Isabella Beeton), Ian Kerr (G. K. Chesterton), Marie Luise Knott (Hannah Arendt), Hermione Lee (Virginia Woolf), Deborah Lutz (the Brontës), Rebecca Mead (George Eliot), Michael Mott (Thomas Merton), Adam Nicholson (Homer), Hazel Rowley (Simone de Beauvoir and Jean-Paul Sartre), Fiona Sampson (Mary Shelley), Miranda Seymour (Mary Shelley), James Shapiro (William Shakespeare), Michael Slater (Charles Dickens), Jane Smiley (Charles Dickens), Ilan Stavans (Miguel de Cervantes), Paul Strohm (Geoffrey Chaucer), John Stubbs (John Donne), John Sutherland (the Brontës), Claire Tomalin (Jane Austen and Charles Dickens), Maisie Ward (G. K. Chesterton), W. H. Wilde (Mary Gilmore),

Garry Willis (G. K. Chesterton), A. N. Wilson (Leo Tolstoy), Emily Wilson (Seneca).

I am grateful also to the many people who have supported and encouraged this book. They include Janet Canny, Daryl Barclay, Brenda Niall, Alice Power, Anna Straford, Jacinta Sheridan, Tony Flynn, Peter Bishop, Ian Nott, Ross Jones and my redoubtable agent, Clare Forster, from Curtis Brown. I could not have had a better team than the one at Text Publishing, especially Michael Heyward and my editor, David Winter, whose enthusiasm for the book helped me find the motivation to see it through. Above all, my gratitude to the wondrous folk who are prepared to share their house with too many books and too few shelves: Jenny, Benedict, Jacob and Clare.